Memoirs of An Old Sweat

by ***DOUG SMITH***

Published by Doug Smith & Co. Ltd., Burrard Building, Vancouver, B.C.
Printed by Evergreen Press Limited, 1070 S.E. Marine Drive, Vancouver.

Table of Contents

TABLE OF CONTENTS (Continued)

Introduction

By JOHN HUNDEVAD

Editor-in-Chief, The Legionary

IT was back in 1946 that I first met Doug Smith when, as a young Army captain fresh home from the wars, he joined the Dominion Headquarters staff of the Canadian Legion in Ottawa as public relations officer.

It did not take me long to realize that Doug had capabilities beyond those of an ordinary P. R. O. His contagious optimism and buoyant sense of humour, plus the ability to express his thoughts vividly on paper, made him a born story-teller—comparable to, yet different in many respects from those other great story-tellers who were monthly contributors to "The Legionary" for many years: Colonel "Jock" Murray (The Orderly Sergeant) and Lieutenant-Colonel Doug Macbeth (Remember When . . . ?). And so, I invited Doug Smith to write a monthly column for "The Legionary". Published under the heading "The Observation Post", it has appeared in every issue of the national magazine of the Royal Canadian Legion ever since the first instalment was printed in January, 1947. Even though Doug has long since left the Legion's Dominion Command for the greener fields of advertising and business promotion, he never fails to produce his monthly budget of wit and whimsicality for "The Legionary".

Now comes this fine collection of World War II service yarns—the pick of the lot written by Doug Smith over the past 15 years for "The Legionary". It is no exaggeration to say that they supply, in book form, an antidote to the stresses and strains of the Cold War existence which this generation is compelled to lead. But they do more than that. To ex-servicemen, whether young or old, the chief emotion they stir is nostalgia—a nostalgia for the days when one got pretty close to life and met one's fellow men on terms that made for candour and unaffectedness unknown before or since. These men, these comrades-in-arms, told yarns, exchanged badinage, recited anecdotes, recalled adventure and, in spontaneous outbursts of wisdom, coined many an unforgettable retort.

It is to the everlasting credit of Doug Smith that, in his own inimitable style, he has immortalized these men through his "Observation Post" in "The Legionary"; and now that, through his own initiative and resourcefulness, they are being made available in permanent form, it is my hope that Legion members and war veterans everywhere will buy this unique volume. I feel certain the book will be treasured beyond measure by all whose own experiences touched upon its contents, and that it will also bring a more balanced understanding to those who have not had the privilege of knowing the comradeship of camp and billet.

Legion House,

Ottawa,

September, 1961.

Top Secret

YOU fellas ever think back and wonder whatever became of some special bloke that you knew in the Services? Someone you had a great liking for but somehow along the line you just drifted apart?

There must be thousands of such "lost chums" around the country. I know of at least ten characters I would dearly love to meet again.

One of those jokers is Chuck Jones. Not that we were exactly blood brothers. Outside of using the same gun-cleaning rags we never "buddy-buddied" around together. Yet he was a bloke that I liked to have around.

Some fellas like types like themselves. Me, I like characters. Perhaps that makes me one. I don't know, but I do know that Chuck was a character and I liked him.

The reason Chuck comes so vividly to mind this time of the year speaks for itself. Anybody who was in Normandy around June '44 sort of thinks back on that as being an outstanding time in his life.

For Chuck it was not only outstanding; it was supremely eventful — a time he and his family will remember for the next fifty years.

There wasn't much in the way of humour in the Normandy landings. The closest to it came from that old crack which you heard everywhere, "Is your journey really necessary?"

Courseulles was the spot where Chuck landed. As part of the headquarters company he set up shop in a fortified house near the railway station by the inlet.

To say there was confusion in the area would be putting it mildly. Two English navy types sightseeing ashore, believe it or not, tendered our hero a snort of true Navy rum.

I'm afraid that this was Chuck's undoing. In company with his new-found friends he went searching for more cups of "Oh Be Joyful". They came upon their doom in the cellar of an abandoned chateau recently used as a German officers' mess.

There, to their delirious joy, were shelves upon shelves of liqueurs, wines, champagnes and hogsheads of apple cider.

Within the hour Chuck was, as they say in the courts, "non compis mentis" — or, as we would say, "out like a light".

His two friends, in not much better shape, rather than abandon him, smuggled him in the dark of night aboard their craft.

Poor Chuck. Hours later he came to with a throbbing noggin' only to find himself back to the very spot he had left some time ago — the bustling port of Portsmouth.

Now this might not have been so bad if Chuck had been prepared to leave well enough alone.

The fact that he was absent from his unit phased him a trifle. But what influenced him even more was that Portsmouth is but a scant sixty or seventy miles from Brighton. And in Brighton was the young lass he had recently married.

Hours later, with the help of an Army Service Corps lorry driver who almost snatched the Swastika armband Chuck bribed him with, he arrived in Brighton.

I don't know exactly how his wife felt when she saw Chuck standing in the door. According to him later, it went something like this:

Chuck: "Howdy Floss, sweetheart."

Floss: "CHUCK! ! ! migawd, I thought you was on the invasion!"

Chuck: "I was and I still am. No time to explain now, ducks, Get up them stairs."

We now skip back to Portsmouth several hours later.

In the hustle and bustle of the sausage machine it was not too difficult for Chuck to tie in with supplies and wend his way back again.

Y'know, it's funny, but chaps never see themselves as others do. To Chuck is was the funniest thing in the world to find that he had been posted as "missing."

Good thing it was too. You could never get away with being missing in England, what with roll-calls, lights out, etcetera.

"Where the bloody hell you been, Jones?" yells the C.S.M.

"Got myself lost, s'hunt-major. Took the wrong turn in the road and got myself behind the Jerry lines. Had to hole up until the way was cleared," Chuck lied cheerfully.

Like all good sergeant-majors his reply was typical: "Pull another stupid trick like that and you'll get your bloody head shot off. Serve you muckin' well right too."

And that was that in the hectic chaos of June, 1944.

Time rolls along and we now find ourselves around March of '45 bogged down around Emmerich.

This was indeed a moist time of the season. Just outside of Emmerich the 3rd Division boys had posted a sign:

"Come in and look around,
The Water Rats have cleared the town."

Chuck by now was no longer the carefree bloke we used to know back in the U.K. Snarly, fidgety and jumpy he hung around each day practically strangling the postal clerk if no mail arrived for him.

We sort of figured that the show was getting him down. The final tip-off came when he turned down a 72-hour pass to Brussels. The idea that any bloke would turn down a leave in Brussels convinced all that Chuck had truly flipped his lid.

"Savin' my leaves for somethin' better," was all Chuck would mutter.

Then came the payoff. A letter from England. Chuck read the letter once, turned beet-red, let out a holler and made a bee-line for the adjutant's tent.

"Sir," says he, all out of breath, "permission requested for compassionate leave."

"Yeah?" says the harrassed and bored adjutant who up to this time had heard more tales of woe than a bill collector. "What is it now? Go ahead and spill it. No, don't tell me — just let me guess. Let me see now. . . Your mother is dying? . . . Your father is going to lose his farm unless you get home? . . . A civilian is planning to run away with your wife?"

"No, sir," blurts out Chuck. "My wife just had twins and they want me home for the christening."

The adjutant lowers his lids like a hooded cobra about to strike. "Hmmm, very interesting, very interesting indeed, Jones. Your request stimulates my curiosity. Now may I ask you a few questions?"

"Sir, you may indeed," says Chuck.

"Well, then," continues the adjutant, "let me refresh my memory, and correct me if I am wrong."

"You arrived in Europe with this unit approximately what date?"

" 'Twas in June, 1944, sir," says Chuck.

"And what time of the year is it now, Jones?" queried the adjutant.

"March, 1945, sir," says Chuck.

"And," continues the adjutant slowly and maliciously, "can you tell me the length of time it takes a woman to have a baby?"

"Nine months, sir" says Chuck, and then a cold sweat begins to break out all over his body.

What to him had been a lark last summer now begins to look like a horse of a different colour. It dawns on him that leaving the theatre of war without permission can be nastily listed as desertion. And for such they have things like firing squads, etcetera.

Rising in wrath the adjutant smacks the table with his ham hand and roars, "I've had about enough of your nonsense, Jones. I have heard some cock and bull stories in my time, but this one plain insults my intelligence. And I do not like to be insulted. Do you hear me?"

"Oh yes, sir, indeed I do, sir," murmurs Chuck in a very, very low voice.

"Then get the hell out of here before I throw you out!" bellows the adjutant. With that he leans out of his tent and shouts: "S'Hunt

Major . . . S'HUNT MAJOR! Give this man some useful work to do and keep him out of my sight for the duration of this war!"

Poor Chuck. I find it hard to believe that somewhere in Canada today he is a hard-working father with a set of twins seventeen years of age born under circumstances that can only be listed as — Top Secret.

Last of the Big Time Spenders

IT was a pulsating heart that beat beneath my Sunday suit as I knocked on the hotel room door. Behind that door was my old buddy of army days, Dusty Miller, whom I hadn't seen in thirteen long years.

"Come on in, and don't break down the bloody door!" roared Dusty as he stood there as big, red-headed and freckled as ever. After the usual bear hugs, back slaps and "Boy! you look great", Dusty broke open a bottle of cognac.

Man! it was good to sniff the aroma of that potent cognac. One whiff brought back a thousand memories. "Thought you'd like it," boomed Dusty. "Figured if we was goin' to have a reunion we might as well do it up brown."

I closed my eyes. I hadn't had cognac like this in years. At nearly eight bucks a bottle, who has? It was then that I looked around the room. But it wasn't just a hotel room. It was a spacious suite.

"You in the chips, Dusty?" I asked.

"Guess you could call it that, Smitty," says he. "This dump runs me twenty-five bucks a day. But what t'hell, it's only money."

I looked at Dusty hard to spot any phony bragadaccios. Then it all came back to me. This was still the same old Dusty. Money never had meant anything to him. It flowed through his fingers like water, and when it was gone he had the happy knack of going out and getting more . . . lots of it.

Six cognacs and two cigars later Dusty told me how he was making money, spending money, losing money and making more money again.

"I watch for the frontiers," says Dusty.

"Frontiers?" says I, blankly.

"Yea, frontiers," says Dusty. "I'm a peddler, Smitty. A real down to earth grubbing peddler."

Still I couldn't grasp how a peddler could rate a layout like this hotel suite.

"Well," says Dusty patiently, "I follow the frontiers. Whenever I hear of a big strike or a big project somewhere, that's where I head for. And the farther away it is, the better I like it.

"Timing is everything," says Dusty. "First you let the guys get to work for awhile, collect some pay, and then you move in before the place has a chance to be settled and the storekeepers open shop!"

"But," says I, "if the storekeepers aren't there, how can you manage to open shop and lug all the goods around?"

"My poor young man," says Dusty as if explaining the facts of life to a child. "My whole travelling kit ain't more than one small valise."

"The pack rats," he snorted contemptuously, "lug in the boots, socks and underwear. Me, I deal strictly in high class merchandise, watches and rings."

"I made ten thousand bucks at Kitimat before the storekeepers moved in. Then I hightailed it for Labrador and cleaned up another five thousand on the railway job in two months, but it was too bloody cold there, so I pulled out."

"My biggest killing, though, was when they was building the big natural gas pipeline in Western Canada. Man, that was a dreamboat! I'm telling you, Smitty, there was welders there in the bush what with double time was making three hundred bucks a week, and nothing to spend it on. Watches that cost me thirty bucks wholesale raised one hundred bucks. I sold eighty in one week."

I could only gape. This was big-time money that made my little pay cheque seem like pop-corn spending.

Then I got to reflecting. Time flashed by and no longer did it seem strange to me. For Dusty was an operator. A real operator. Never crooked, but just born with the talent for spotting a chance to make dough. And enough of it so he could relax, smoke big cigars and not do a tap of work for months.

My first observation of Dusty's financial genius came around August, '44. We were rummaging through an abandoned German Q.M. store close to the Fontaine d'Arlette, which lies below the Castle Falaise on the cliff above.

There was the usual junk scattered around. Nothing worth taking as far as I could see. No Lugers, no binoculars. I casually pocketed a few swastika badges, an SS hat and prepared to leave.

"On your feet, Dusty," says I. "Let's see if we can round up a few kegs of cider."

"Hold your hosses, laddie," says Dusty, loading his haversack with dozens of swastika belt buckles, storm trooper badges and several Nazi flags.

"Holy cow!" I yelled. "What in hell you gonna do with all that junk?"

"You leave it to ole Dusty, pal," says he with a big smirk. "I ain't quite certain about it yet. But I got ideas."

I shrugged and waited as he loaded up. Dusty was either going loco or else the Calvados had got him.

I gave it no further thought. Exactly one year later I was to learn from Dusty a few facts of life.

The war was over and here were thousands of troops in Holland, idle and with only mischief on their minds.

So the Brass did the proper thing. They ladled out ten-day passes. Both Dusty and I were due for a leave. There was only one hitch. We were dead broke. Even my next pay was spoken for. I had fallen for my old weakness of trying to draw to an inside straight and missed.

"Smitty," says Dusty, "let's go anyhow."

"Yeah," says I, "and what do we use for money? Woodbines? They got them in the U.K. already yet."

Those were the days when with only faith and a prayer you did things first and worried about them afterwards. Between us and our friends we raised ten quid and away we went.

Winging over the Channel in a reliable old Dakota we soon landed at the London airport.

"Anything to declare? Cognac, perfume, silk?" asks the customs officer.

"Nothing," says Dusty nonchalantly, "'cept a few war souvenirs for the kids."

The customs officer, an old sweat from the First War, gives Dusty a knowing wink. "For the kiddies, eh? An' maybe for a bit o' fluff too, eh, Canada?"

"Now there you've got something, mate," replies Dusty, returning the knowing wink with a sexy leer.

Only Dusty could do it. Me, I would have been apprehended, searched and locked up in the Tower of London.

A few hours later we were checking in at the Regent Palace Hotel. "How's about chances for a suite, friend?" says Dusty to the harrassed-looking room clerk.

Before he had a chance to open his mouth and give us the brush-off, I heard the rustle of a pound note as Dusty slipped it into his hand. Man! did that clerk's face ever change. "Yes — sir, yes — sir, just a moment, sir, I'll see what I can do for you sir."

Five minutes later, ensconced in a regal suite, I blasted out at Dusty. "Man alive! You gone crazy? Here we are with ten quid to our name and you slip that pimp a whole pound when we should be shacking up at the Beaver Club."

"Easy boy, easy does it," soothed Dusty. "It's now we go to work."

An hour later I twigged Dusty's devious mind as we made for the Snakepit, a crowded walk-down cellar taken over by the Americans.

Quietly sipping his gin and tonic, Dusty finally moved into action. "First you gotta get someone to do your advertising," he says. "And it must be one of their own kind. Always get me a lippy, nervous, talkative type. They spread real good."

Within minutes he had his mark selected. Casually fingering a Nazi belt buckle, he let a lippy GI nearby pick it up and fondle the merchandise. You could see the look of desire in the guy's eyes. A few remarks by Dusty that the buckle could be his for free if he rounded up a few friends was enough to set him moving.

In jig-time a drooling group of souvenir hunters were pressing around. Fellas, I am telling you that I have seen bargain-crazy women at sales, but they were tranquilized infants compared to this mob.

This was manna from Heaven. All of those GI's were chairborne wallahs who had never moved out of London. To get an honest to goodness Nazi swastika to take back to the States with them was something out of this world.

As fast as he could dish them out and I could make change, Dusty disposed of sixty belt buckles at a pound apiece! S.S. badges followed at the same rate, plus other sundries. Then came his *piece de resistance* as he casually displayed a five-foot Nazi flag.

"How much am I offered?" says Dusty. Before anyone could get a word in a large sergeant with a Texan drawl pushed forward. "Ah don't want to argue with nobody," he says, "but ah wants that flag. How about a hundred dollars good U.S. money."

That started the pandemonium. The flag finally went for thirty quid.

One hundred and fifty pounds later I just sprawled, mentally exhausted, in our sumptuous suite at the Regent Palace.

It was a leave to remember as ten days later we flew back to Amsterdam . . . dead broke!

Dusty, old boy, you were worth knowing. Believe me!

Special Assignment

IN the early part of the Last Great Unpleasantness, round about this time of the year, I was stationed at National Defence Headquarters in Ottawa and immersed in a very serious problem.

In my tiny cubicle in the War House on Albert Street I was endeavouring to decide whether I should fill out certain forms in quadruplicate or chuck them in the basket and go for a beer at the Lord Elgin Hotel around the corner.

As the hour was a quarter to five this was a serious decision to have to make. After tossing for the best out of three, the Lord Elgin finally won. Slipping on my greatcoat I just about had it made to the door when a voice behind me barks, "You there! The Old Man wants to see you on the double!"

For six days in a row the Old Man never as much as knows that I am alive. Now, a few minutes before quitting time, he want to see me on the double. Gad, what a system!

"Smith," says the Old Man. "Tomorrow at 1400 hours" — not two o'clock, mind you; it has to be 1400 hours — "the Jack Benny troupe will be here as part of a Victory Bond tour. It is our assignment to see that they are looked after every minute they are here and sent away again safely. I will look after Mr. Benny and Mary Livingstone myself. I want you to take care of Rochester."

"Now then," he continues, "here is their itinerary. At 1600 hours they are to be at Rideau Hall to meet the Earl of Athlone and Princess Alice. At 1730 hours they are to be on Parliament Hill to meet Mr. Mackenzie King, Defence Minister Ralston, and other members of the cabinet. At 2100 hours they will be at Lansdowne Park for a show, and at 2330 hours they are to be safely aboard their train. You will stay with Rochester every blessed single minute of his visit here. Never, never, never let him out of your sight. Understand?"

Promptly at 1400 hours the next day I met the troupe, bedded them down at the Chateau Laurier, shined their shoes, wiped their noses, and flushed the toilet for them. When the army lays down a V.I.P. itinerary, you, brother fighting soldier, are nothing, nothing at all — believe me. The V.I.P. is Aly Khan, Genghis Khan and the Lord High Executioner all rolled into one.

Rochester, bless his soul, presented a few problems. Everytime I tried to hurry him up he would raise a protesting hand: "Ah'll be right with you in jest a minute, boss — jest as soon as ah finishes this heah bourbon transfusion."

"Rochester," says I, "my job is to get you to Rideau Hall and safely away. If I don't do this my Old Man will have me peeling potatoes for the duration of this ruddy war." I then went on to explain how the Earl of Athlone was a very dignified gentleman and Princess Alice a perfect little lady. And so, would he please, just for once, play this straight, and no shenanigans.

I'll say this much for Rochester, he performed nobly. He gave a polite little bow to Princess Alice and shook the Governor-General's hand in manly fashion. We then moved along the line and I made a bee-line for the flunkey in the white coat ladling out glasses of Oh Be Joyful.

Several free loads later I was startled by the Old Man pinching my shoulder and saying, "The escort is ready outside. Pick up Rochester and let's go."

"Right away, sir," says I, and around I look for Rochester. Jack Benny, Mary Livingstone and Dennis Day I see, but no Rochester. Feeling a little panicky I searched for him in the spacious rooms. Still no sign of the honoured guest.

Down in the doorway, looking impatiently at his watch and beckoning me to hurry along, was the Old Man. The provost officer was there, the staff cars were outside and the motor cycle escort were warming up their machines.

Beads of perspiration dripped down my back. I had committed the cardinal sin. I had been given an order *never* to let Rochester out of my sight and this I had ignored. The thought that a man could go astray while at Rideau Hall never occurred to me. But then I didn't know my Rochester.

By now I had broken into a desperate dog-trot searching the rooms, corridors and washrooms. Still no Rochester.

To say that my Old Man was black in the face is the master understatement of the year. He was alternately black, red and white according to the bloodstreams rushing to and from his face.

In desperation I scurried downstairs into the servants' quarters. Surely he couldn't be down here? But then I heard that blessed, melodious and husky voice! Looking into the scullery I saw a sight that I'll never forget. There on the floor sat Rochester surrounded by four liveried flunkeys, with Rochester rolling the dice and moaning, "C'mon, baby, papa needs new shoes."

To my desperate pleadings to "please, please, come along" he paid scant interest, so intent was he on rolling his point.

Then the climax came. In the doorway there appeared no less a personage than the Major Domo of Rideau Hall. A gentleman's gentleman he was, of some three score years and ten, who had served royalty and vice-royalty for a lifetime.

To him the fact that a guest would be in the servants' quarters was something fantastically unbelievable. But for a guest not only to be there, but sitting on the floor playing crap with the flunkeys was just too much for the poor man.

With the blood drained from his face he coughed and croaked, "I beg your pardon, sir . . . I BEG your pardon."

Undaunted, Rochester looked up from his squatting position and with a cheery wave of his hand said, "Say theah, boy, do you all think His Highness would like to come down and roll me for a few provinces?"

Weakly I staggered up with him to the motor escort and cringed in a corner under my Old Man's burning eyes.

A Salute to The Senior Class 1914–18

EACH time the mail comes up with the rations there is always a letter from some Old Sweat asking for more anecdotes about the First Great Nastiness.

This got me to thinking as it presented a bit of a problem. Just about that time of the century I was busily engaged burping a milk formula instead of *vin rouge*. So I am afraid my memory of the 1914-18 fracas is none too good.

On the other hand I got to talking with a few of the Old Contemptibles who gave me enough insight to write a few lines of nostalgia that might be of interest to you lovers of Tickler's Jam.

The old 1st Division cherish their memories of Boiz Grenier, the piggeries at Plug Street, the Petit Douve, Wulverghem and so on. The 2nd Div. have theirs of Reninghelst, Dickebusch and the Brasserie.

The Third recall Locre, Kemmel Hill and Dranoutre and the Fourth retain ancient memories of the Somme.

It might also be of interest to the young 'uns of World War II to learn a little more how their fathers slugged it out under conditions most unbearable.

This is a mythical letter I have put together that might have been written from France to a soldier friend in Canada.

Dear Joe:

Censorship forbids me to say where we are. All I can say is that the route marches at Valcartier were soft compared to hobbling over these cobble stones.

To make matters worse our Canadian army boots have now been changed to British issue and brother they weigh about five pounds each. The army says that with the heels and soles all ironclad they will last forever. This I can well believe. It's only the longevity of my blisters that worries me.

I'll say this much though for the British they got a dry sense of humour. The first day we arrived at the front in a blithering sleet storm a British sergeant shouts at us, "Cheer up lads, I've always 'eard as 'ow the first seven years of war as is the worst."

The Front is a juicy spot indeed. It is so wet that I keep giving Bill long looks each day to make certain he isn't growing a tail and reverting to a tadpole.

We have just taken over a German trench and inherited their lice which are both regimented and patriotic. They march up your back in lines of four and down the other side without breaking ranks. The way in which they cling to your clothes assures you of their patriotism and their desire never to leave you.

I must say it is summat noisy here. The Boches send over long shells called Coal Boxes or Jack Johnsons. This is a 5.9 howitzer shell which you hear a long way off like an express train and then explodes like thunder throwing up large volumes of thick black smoke.

Then they have high explosive shells named Wooley Bears which explode in the air throwing great clouds of dense white and yellow smoke. The boys have made up a jingle about them which goes something like this:

Woof, Woof, wooley bear, whizzing high and low,
Making little soldier-boys hug the parado,
Bursting here, bursting there, detonations mighty,
Strewing iron all around and sending blokes to Blighty.

The Boche also has an aerial torpedo which comes across at night with a trail of sparks and falls with the darndest noise you ever heard. The blighters have a rudder on them which makes them swerve before they drop and you can't tell for the life of you which way it will fall.

Joe, I hope you will excuse my writing this with the stub of an indelible pencil, but it isn't very practical to carry a bottle of ink in your knapsack.

Please keep on writing your chatty letters to me. You have no idea how important mail from home means over here. Each time the mail arrives there is a real rush for the guy with the letters. I have seen pretty tough blokes turn their heads and almost cry when they found there was no mail for them.

We do have moments though that make life bearable. One of the brightest spots is the appearance of our padre Canon Scott. Some time ago we were all billeted near an old chateau at Ecoivres.

The padre held one of his meetings which is always well attended. This particular night he was going to read to us any questions we might like to put down on paper and the padre would give us an answer.

Believe me the boys used to throw some real slick ones at him. But he never batted an eye or turned a hair. This one however was a real shocker. It was obvious that the good man as he opened the envelope had not read the question beforehand. He read it out loud and it went like this:

Dear Padre:

I am going to ask you a question which has been a load to my little bit of mental capacity for a period of months. Often have I woke up in the old dugout, my hair standing straight up and one eye looking straight into the eyeball of the other trying to obtain an answer to this burning question. I have kept my weary vigil over the parapet at night, with my rifle in one hand and a couple of bombs in the other, and two or three in my pocket, and still I am pondering over this burning question. I will now ask you the question, "When do you think this God dam war will be over, eh?"

The padre rocked for a second almost as shocked as we were. But only for a second. His head reared back and he lead the biggest roar of laughter heard this side of Berlin. No wonder we all adore him.

Another little funny incident I must tell you about is the time we were in the grounds of an old farm house. The Boche were still there but we managed to drive them out in the fields while we took over the stables.

This doesn't sound like much until I tell you that our section of the stable was the pig sty and the stench was something awful. It may have been a dead pig nearby so we argued whether it was the pig or the pig manure making the smell. However Bill solved the riddle with his, "Naw, it ain't one or the other, I think it's the officers mess."

After that remark things didn't seem too bad at all.

Well Joe this bit of candle is flickering mighty low so I guess I will sign off now.

All the best,

George.

Somefink abart the Wrens

BY golly, fellas, I am in the throes of what the movie moguls call a dilemma. A few months ago, in response to a request for a few words about the lassies in uniform, I wrote about a maiden in khaki named Molly McGee. Now comes an urgent signal from overseas, saying that the maiden in question was not a regular collector of His Majesty's pounds, shillings and spam.

The signal flashed from Kingston-on-Thames, Surrey, reads as follows:

"You 'orrible Canadian, promising us a story abart women and turns arter be abart a war correspondent (female). You ain't a Canuck if yer don't print somefink abart Wrens. Love, good wishes and appreciation of Observation Post and all Canucks of 1939 - 45."

Signed: The Wrens — BLACK STOCKING BRIGADE.

The signal from the Wrens was written on a postcard showing a picture of Wimborne Minster. Across it was printed, "WHERE THE YANKS WERE." It seems to me that I jeeped through Wimborne one Sunday afternoon. Correct me, you Grable-bodied seamen, but didn't the Yanks have an airforce station nearby? And didn't you Wrens have some nesting boxes in that area alongside a bird cage?

Now, then, I ask you fellas, what does a bloke after thirteen years remember about Wrens other than that they were purty, chirpy, and did a bang-up job in helping to win the war.

However, at the risk of being wren-pecked I dug into my wartime diary and discovered a few mentions of pleasant association with the lovable wearers of pusser's lisle.

My first contact with a member of the Women's Royal Naval Service was on my second trip overseas. Aboard "The Lizzie" we were ruminating in the lounge, staring at the ceiling, biting our nails and, at this point, bored to tears. There was the usual gabble-gabble of a large crowd when suddenly it tuned down to a dead quiet. There, standing in the doorway, were no less than six pink-cheeked, flashing-eyed members of the W.R.N.S.

Fellas, I can assure you it was an electrifying moment. Here, herded together were umpteen thousand virile young Canadian bloods, ne'er dreaming there was a lass around for thousands of miles.

To adequately describe the scene is beyond my scope and ability. As I said before, there was a quietening calm — like the lull before a storm. Then the mad scramble began to offer seats to the somewhat startled young ladies in navy blue. When the dust had settled, thirteen soldiers were found crushed underneath, with eight suffering from contusions, abrasions, shock and bleeding eyeballs.

I can tell you blokes that that there room perked up something fierce. Guys who ten minutes before were looking at life with glazed eyes hauled out pocket combs, buttoned their tunics and did their damndest to look like Clark Gable on vacation.

It was quite a triumph for these Wrens to be at sea. The navy brass, reluctantly accepting the fact that women might have a place in the show, were adamant about them not going to sea. However, they got there. But before they could do so and be officially recognized, an Act had to be passed by Parliament.

I believe the young women served aboard as scribes or killick scribes. Anyhow, it didn't matter whether they were ratings or rear-admirals. The position these young ladies held in His Majesty's Forces did not visibly affect the ardent attention paid them by that Canadian draft.

I was told that these six Wrens were the first to go to sea in World War II. For posterity, I find the names of three of them recorded in my diary. They are Joan Stonehouse, Joan Penney and Alys Murray. I wonder where they are today?

In the last show not too many Canadians in khaki escorted Wrens about Lunnon town. The Navy might have the rep of being the Silent Service, but when it came to protecting its Wrens, man, were they ever vigilant! Everytime a good-looking Wren was seen near Mayfair, alongside was sure to be a naval escort.

However, there was one time when I was alone in a compartment of Jenny's aboard the Lover's Leap. To you fragile-minded sweats, the Lover's Leap was the first early morning train from Waterloo to Portsmouth.

It was my one moment of glory with the navy girls. They fussed over me and I was the complete centre of attraction. However, upon reflection it now occurs to me that the honest-to-goodness carton of Canadian cigarettes which I carried may have had considerable bearing on my popularity.

If my memory serves me correctly, members of the Women's Royal Naval Service served in the 1914-18 war too. In the intervening peacetime years they were disbanded and did not officially come into being again until 1939. Consequently, while many R.N. professional officers accepted the presence of the Wrens, even allowing them to go sea, the sacrosanct spot where no woman was allowed was the bar. She might come into the premises on specified occasions, but standing at the bar was strictly out-of-bounds.

However, even the stoutest fortress must sometimes be challenged. At a certain hallowed navy spot in England a lonely Wren sat at a table nursing her diminishing drink and deciding that it was "a long ship". For the edification of you landlubbers, "a long ship" means it's one helluva long interval between the first drink and the offer of a second.

Fed up with waiting, the Three-O picked up her glass, marched up to the bar, elbowed two oak-leaved officers aside, plunked two-and-six on the counter and in a determined voice said, "Gin and Tonic, please . . . double."

There was a shocked and horrible silence.

"There'll be blood for breakfast," gasped an awed lieutenant.

They tell me that at that precise moment Lord Mountbatten, visiting faraway Sanctuary Buildings, froze dead in his tracks. "What ever is wrong, sir," said an aide. "You look pale, sir. Are you ill?"

"I don't know," replied Mountbatten. "I've just had a premonition that something terrible has happened. The Navy may never be the same again."

Well, sir, when that Wren Joan of Arc plunked her two-and-six on the bar, there was a rustling of navy lace and a bristling of navy beards that supplied enough electricity to light a heavy cruiser.

Triumphant, the Wren sailed back to her table, flaunting the green and white gin pennant for all Wrens to come aboard and join her.

Well, Jenny, that is my pleasant little memory of association with you during 1939 - 45. As much as I would like to flog the clock, warm the bell and make my leave seem longer, I must be away to catch the Jellicoe Express.

So I will turn it up at that. And in reply to your fond thoughts for all Canucks I would like to sign off on their behalf with some wartime greetings of S.W.A.K. — T.W.M.A., or better still, B.O.L.T.O.P.!

Aye, aye, ma'am. See you at Aggy Westons.

We Shoot a Collaborator

YOU fellas may remember it was around September '44 that we had the Hun on the run and the rat-race across France had begun.

I was sitting in my "requisitioned" armchair in Caen uncorking a bottle of my favourite Chablis when a runner bursts in saying, "The Old Man wants to see you, and I'd say he ain't exactly smilin' at life in general."

"Blow me down," I muttered. "What in blazes is this war coming to when a fella can't have a moment of privacy to hisself and enjoy a small portion of Chablis?"

Corking my bottle I shambled over to the Old Man's tent. He looks up darkly. "Smith," says he, "I have just returned from Army. They tell me that the troops have not seen a copy of *The Maple Leaf* in days. What in hell are you doing with the papers — saving them for Christmas wrappers?"

Terribly uncouth fellow, was my Old Man. No niceties about him at all.

"I want you," he says, deliberate-like, "I want you to get up and off your big fat pratt, take a thirty-hundredweight and get the hell up to the front and see what gives with our papers."

I gulped. The man was serious. He actually wanted me to go up there where they were shooting real bullets at people. By gad, I'd obey the chap, but my member of parliament would surely hear from me about it.

"And," yells he, "this time when you take that truck up I don't want to find it full of casks of cider. This bloody unit is beginning to smell like a distillery."

You fellas see what I mean. Of all the ungratitude! Two months ago when I risked life and limb to supply him with cider, calvados and cases of Chablis I was a ruddy hero. Now, I was a lazy bum who was stenching up the joint with my unsavoury wares.

Sherman was right when he said, "War is Hell!"

Well, you blokes know the story of the Great Confusion. The Mortain salient had been reduced to the Falaise-Argentan pocket and this pocket had dwindled to the Trun gap and then it had been closed.

The orders were to get to the Seine without delay and General Crerar wheeled his forces east. Even before Falaise was captured, the

1st Canadian Corps had begun to wheel east and it was in high gear when we started from Trun.

I soon found out why the troops weren't getting *The Maple Leaf*. The units never stayed long enough in one place to catch up with it. Headquarters changed sometimes twice a day and you could never find out exactly where the next location was.

As one brigadier put it when asked where his divisional headquarters was, "Divisional headquarters? How the hell should I know. I can't even locate my own regiments."

"Hmmmm," says my Old Man when I broke the news to him. "It looks like we will have to move out of Caen and print the paper some place else. Get going again and see if you can find a town big enough and close enough where we can set up shop."

Now this posed a problem. To do our kind of business you had to parlay with the Frenchman who owned a printing plant. Just "taking over" as we did in Caen was not the accepted procedure any more, and, to make matters worse, at this point in the game most of our parlay-vooing was limited to *"une verre du vin, s'il vous plait"* . . . and *"cigarette pour papa"*.

Attached to our unit by his own adoption was a fast-talking little Norman named Gabby. We never knew his real name, but as he talked a blue streak all the time, we nicknamed him Gabby. To my knowledge he never got paid for interpreting but seemed to be happy to eat our rations, smoke our cigarettes and wave grandiosely to the villagers as he drove past them in a Canadian army vehicle.

Frankly, he spoke terrible English and understood it even less; but he put on such a good show that, at least in comparison with our parlayvooing the ding-dong, he was a Rhodes scholar.

Around the end of August I set off with Gabby, a cameraman and a driver to find a new home for the unit.

I believe it was August 30 on a drizzly afternoon that the North Nova Scotia Highlanders, the Highland Light Infantry and the Stormont, Dundas and Glengarry Highlanders entered Rouen.

I followed them at a safe and respectful distance.

The liberation of Rouen was one of those stirring events which were to be duplicated in Paris, Brussels, Antwerp and other points. Thousands upon thousands of people jammed the streets as our convoys rumbled over the cobble-stones. Vehicles were festowed with bright coloured dahlias and gladioli, and wine bottles and cigarettes were exchanged in wild confusion.

But Rouen was not to be the resting place of the Canadians. The 2nd Division swung towards Dieppe, 40 miles due north, and the 3rd and 4th Divisions, without resting after their 70-mile advance from Trun, were ordered to go on to the Somme.

Meanwhile a little reconnaissance was in order. Turning to Gabby, our cameraman Jake pipes up: "*Mon ami,* we need a little action around here. We should shoot a few scenes of collaborators and local F.F.I. See what you can round up for us."

"*Certainement,* with *joyeux,*" cries Gabby in that mixed-up lingo he called English.

I'll swear he wasn't gone twenty minutes when he returns with as fierce a looking group as war could collect together. Hustled along between the F.F.I. group were three abject and frightened collaborators.

"*Voila!*" cries Gabby. "We 'ave ze collaborateurs. Now we shoot dem, like you say." And with that he bangs off rapid fire French to the F.F.I. men who quickly line the poor wretches against a wall and bring their Sten guns to the front.

Horrified, I realized what Gabby had done. He had misinterpreted our Canadian slang for shooting a scene, and all he got out of it was a request to shoot a few collaborators!

It was a contemptuous F.F.I. group that shrugged their shoulders when I explained to them that we merely wished to shoot a few pictures of collaborators with a camera, not with a gun.

As for Gabby, he was crestfallen. I had not merely spoiled his fun but lowered the whole prestige of the Canadian Army as tough fighters in front of his compatriots.

Days later, in great relief, I dumped Gabby at the Belgian border. We had entered a new era, one in which interpreting was not required. Within three months the Canadian troops were expert lingoists.

Everyone agreed that their French and Dutch grammar was atrocious but sufficed, quite sufficed, to successfully request the amenities of life.

It Shouldn't Happen to a Dog

YOU fellows ever been haunted by memories of the past? Ever wake up wondering what has happened to an old girl friend you once knew in London, Brussels, Antwerp or Oldenburg?

Me, I'm the unlucky type. I not only get haunted by these memories. I bump into the real McCoy in her scintillating, perfumed flesh.

Fascinating thought, huh? I'll bet you guys are muttering "Lucky dog, wish I could meet some of those pretties from the days of You Know When . . . boy, would I ever have a night on the town!"

Perish the thought, you Lothario's of '44. It's all a pipe dream that turns into a nightmare. Believe me, I know from experience. You see, I wasn't alone when it happened to me . . . the Little Woman was right alongside.

On a rapturous night not so long ago the Little Woman and I were taking in a night at the Press Club. It was one of those evenings when the press boys get together and throw a wing-ding for a visiting celebrity. Reporters are the closest thing in civvy street to servicemen. At the drop of a bottle-opener they can justify a reason for throwing a party.

This Press Club occasion wasn't bad as such do's go. They had the usual gimmicks — a wheel of fortune, crown and anchor, bingo, blackjack with the banker turning up all 21's, plus all the niceties of life guaranteed to separate you from your baby bonus cheque.

To top it all off and to make the separation less painful, a couple of makeshift bartenders were sloshing out tumblers full of "Oh Be Joyful." Yes-sir, the blood was pounding something fierce in the old buck's carcass.

And then amidst all this raucous goings on I ran smack into a pair of eyes. Allow me to inform you gentlemen of the King's Shilling that I had seen those eyes somewhere before. Indeed, I had seen them at very, very close quarters but, where at one time they had thrilled me, they now shocked me into a state of near-epilepsy.

There could be no doubt about it. Those eyes could belong to one and only one gal, namely Diana of the Chelsea Arms. Well, sir, I'm telling you that I right near dropped in my tracks. At any other time I would have welcomed those taunting orbs. But, puhleeze, why did it have to happen just when the Little Woman was standing by?

At first look Diana didn't tumble to the fact that it was me she was seeing. Fellas, I'm telling you this was one time I was happy over that extra thirty pounds, the receding hairline and the comfortable paunch! I reckoned she didn't figure this pudgy civilian to be the one and same rangy elbow-bender of the rum and peppermint heydays.

Now before you blokes start yelling "chicken" in my direction, let me remind you that Diana was something special. There are some old flames that you can walk right up to the Little Woman and give with the old schmaltz, "Darling, I want you to meet Myrtle. Me and Myrtle had a crush on each other at one time, hah, hah, hah!"

Under normal circumstances the women give each other the quick three-second appraisal and figure they no longer have anything to fear. From there on you are home free.

But not so with Diana. She is the kind of a gal that sets the hackles to rise on other women's necks the minute she enters a room. Even in the lush days of free-for-all laughter at the Chelsea-Arms, Diana never clicked with the other gals. She was strictly a lassie who loved men's company and couldn't care less for women's.

Luckily, on this first exchange of glances, the Little Woman was all fevered up holding a ten and an ace in her blackjack hand and waiting to clobber the banker. So me, coward that I am, I give Diana the "I don't know you" casual look and turn my back.

Alongside me was Mike who used to be a war correspondent overseas. Mike had also known Diana as a "good friend". He had wined, dined and danced her all over the night spots of London town. I nudged Mike in the ribs. Out of the corner of my mouth, like only an ex-con or ex-serviceman can mutter, I said, "Don't look now, but Diana of the old Chelsea-Arms is here."

Mike went white as a gin-fizz. "You're kidding," he whispers, giving a nervous side-glance at his wife.

"S'help me, Mike, I'm not. I only wish I was."

Then Mike in a near-panic wheeled around to see for himself. And there, standing not six feet away, was Diana. Seeing the two of us together, a light dawned in her tawny eyes. With her mouth wide open, like Marilyn Monroe, she gushed, "Why Smitty *and* Mike, how simply wonderful to see you again — yak, yak, yak!"

At the sound of that sultry voice both wives wheeled in unison. And there they saw two red-faced, tongue-tied characters trying to stammer out an introduction.

It wasn't necessary. The Little Woman takes one peek at Diana and in one thousandth of a second her warm blue eyes turned into cold agate stone.

Gad, why should a gal like Diana have appeared electric and luscious to you thirteen years ago and now seem hard and flashy? Diana had lost little of her attractiveness, only now the scene had changed. Changed, that is, for us old buckaroos.

Both Mike's wife and mine were coiffured and dressed right smart. But such wholesome perfection was never Diana's strong point. She was dressed for the kill. The deep V-Cleft in her dress looked like the Grand Canyon; her eyes were shadowed with blueing like Jayne Mansfield made up for the cameras, and her eyelashes seemed to be starched straight out.

Diana, bless her, was the only one to hold her nerve. Matter of fact she was all nerve — and gab. "Oh, you simply *must* meet my husband," she gushes. With a deft twist she turns a bloated character away from the bar and says, "Dahling, you *simply* must meet Smitty and Mike. You remember, I told you about them when I had that flat at Chelsea."

Oi, oi, oi, oi! This was going to be grim. And it was. Albert his name was, and pickled to the eyes he was also. "What ho!" he cries. "I'll say I remember those rascals. By gad, you fellows used to throw some smashing bottle-parties in Chelsea. Still talk about them there, they do."

Then he focuses on me, "I say, theah, weren't you the bloke who climbed up Diana's drainpipe the night she lost the key to her apartment?"

What does a guy do, I ask you? Me, I give with a sickly little laugh — heh, heh. And the Little Woman is staring like she is really seeing me for the first time.

They tell me that the nightmare lasted only five minutes and then the exchange broke up. "You must come out and see us sometime," Diana says in parting.

"Yeh, yeh, yeh, sure thing," says I right quickly. "Sure been nice to see you again."

No need to tell you guys that the rest of the night was shot in clammy silence.

The unkindest cut came two weeks later just when I figured I was out of the dog house.

"How about fixing the TV aerial on Saturday," says the Little Woman in a disarming voice.

"Aw heck," says I, "how can I? We haven't got a ladder."

"That shouldn't faze you," she coos. "You're used to shinnying up drainpipes. Why don't you try ours?"

Gadzooks, fellas. You call that cricket? Dashed unsporting, I say.

"Cigarette pour Papa?"

DEAR Mr. Diefenbaker:

Before the High Command makes any decision about shipping Canadian troops overseas in any future war would you please consult me? And before you accept compiled logistics from The Brass would you kindly have a chat with me?

The boys with the war brains will fill both your ears with the need for trucks, tanks, guns and other implements of war. But I will bet you three mild-and-bitters that they will overlook the most important item of all — a secret weapon so necessary that if the troops were to go overseas without it, it would mean disaster.

This, sir, is a harmless little object that contains plenty of fire and smoke. You got it the first time, but in case you didn't, I will tell you. I am referring to that little piece of weed, the soldier's dream, the comforter of lonely men — the lowly cigarette.

Nonsense, says you? My goodness, no, sir. If you will hearken back to your own army days for awhile, it might refresh your memory as to the importance of the humble fag in a soldier's life. Don't you remember crawling back into your trench after a weary patrol? Then, what was the first thing you asked for? Was it a tank? A howitzer? No, sir. You clamped that little white butt between your teeth, took a deep drag, let out a sigh and, come hell or high water, you were your old self once again.

Did you ever notice the look of strain on a wounded man's face as he was carried into a field dressing station? Do you remember what was his first request? Was it for a sixty hundredweight truck? A drum of petrol? No, sir. It was the simple request: "Has anyone got a fag?" Then, have you ever watched the look of relief on his face as he lights up? Believe me, for just a few minutes he is a new man.

I could quote you a hundred different examples about the importance of the "filthy weed" in warfare. People damn it. They swear they will give it up — next week. But whenever you see a soldier, you will see a cigarette.

You still think that it is not important? Then go ahead and take one of our units in Germany and use it as a guinea pig. Cut off the boys' cigarettes, then sit back and await their reaction. Hah, you think you got troubles with the atom bomb! Watch this blast! It will melt the brass off shoulders five thousand miles away! ! !

Wherever the Canadian soldier went in the last two wars, whenever the cheering Europeans clapped their heroes on the back, what was the first thing they asked their liberators? Did they say, "Could I have a rifle?" Or, "You got some money?" No, sir. The first thing you heard was that classic that now should be in all military manuals, "Cigarette for papa?"

The most precious thing in a serviceman's life abroad was his supply of cigarettes. A man might have ninety quid in his paybook, but he was only as rich as the number of fags he possessed. Any guy in the hut with 600 cigarettes would put Aly Khan to shame. He was the most sought-after bloke in the unit. If he was free with his gaspers he could win any popularity contest.

Not only was his supply of cigarettes vital to himself; it also played an important role in the welfare of all other men. Sure, an army marches on its stomach. But that stomach can get mighty tired of a steady diet of dehydrated potatoes and compo rations.

It was surprising during the last war how many units managed to wangle fresh eggs, the odd chicken and fresh vegetables. No, sir, those items did *not* come up with the rations. They were not purchased with shillings, lires, francs, guilders or reichmarks. It was the lowly cigarette that was the accepted currency of the day.

Bank presidents might sweat far into the night trying to devise a stabilized currency for their liberated country. The people looked at the folding stuff with a curled lip. But you should see their faces light up when the cigs were produced. Like magic the hard-to-get items were offered. "You want a Luger?" "Good camera?" "Fresh vegetables?" "Well, how many cigarettes you got?"

Citizens hoarded cigarettes like precious nuggets. Packets changed hands a dozen times in exchange before they would be opened for a smoke. The currency of the country might drop, but the price and demand for cigarettes spiralled.

If you walked into my living room today, sir, you would admire the Dutch paintings on the wall. You would finger the Belgian ornaments with appreciative hands. You would view the lovely French lace on my table with murmurs of "good taste".

How did I acquire such expensive adornments? Not on the King's Shilling, I assure you, but through the kindness of my beloved aunts who kept plying me with cigarettes. Would you be shocked to learn that one cigarette fetched one guilder? And one guilder was worth about forty cents. So, cigarettes — bless their smoldering little rice hides — played an important part in my home life.

Cigarettes, sir, were a great aid to Canadian international relations. They broke more ice than all of the "How to Behave" books you could print.

So you met a Dutchman. He couldn't speak English and the only Dutch words you knew were *schnapps* and *herrenroom*. You gibbished at each other for minutes in hopeless befuddlement. Then you produced a package of cigarettes. You should see the look on that Dutchman's face. He beamed, he glowed and became more mellow than a Zuider Zee cheese. From there on you were in, one hundred percent.

In army personal relations there was a great unwritten code about cigarettes. It was accepted practice to "borrow" another guy's blanket, his gaiters or clean socks. But to lay hands on another's cigarettes was an unforgiveable crime. A crime that was punished, not by any orderly room procedure, but by a complete snubbing from your bunk mates. Those of you who have lived in an army hut know just how cruel and humiliating that punishment can be.

Whenever there was a real shortage among the troops, it was not considered polite to pass your cigarettes around when you took one for yourself. It was figured just plain damn foolishness.

However, I knew one gentleman of the old school, a certain sergeant. He continued to pass his cigarettes around, but he had a levelled .38 in the other hand.

One private ignored the hint and took a cigarette. The sergeant promptly shot him between the eyes.

There wasn't even a court of inquiry. The case was simply written off as "justifiable homicide."

Then I remember one night in Paris when the shortage was really acute. We were in a hotel lobby when the lights went out. A C.W.A.C. was heard to scream. An officer asked if she was being molested.

"Molested, hell!" she stormed. "Some blankety - blank - blank snatched the cigarette out of my mouth."

Ah well, *c'est la guerre*. . .

Cigarette for papa?

Of Madame Declerq and le Capitaine Matthews

I was down in the basement rummaging through an old trunk and enjoying my favourite Sunday afternoon sport of thumbing over old war souvenirs. "What gives down there, Spirit of '39," comes the joshing voice of The Little Woman.

Funny thing about wives. The critters have more insight into a guy's insides than an X-ray machine. Guess that's what happens when two people live together for a long time. Anyhow, l'il ole Blue Eyes has got now so she can spot that far-away look of mine without even turning her head.

She claims and will back it up with arguments that she is certain the happiest days of my life were spent in the services. To which I give vehement denials, although I must confess that I sound less convincing as the years roll along.

Anyhow, as I said before, I was rummaging through my old junk. This battered-up piece of framework is a lulu. It contains everything from hat bands marked "Vlanderen Korps", Swastika badges, German armed forces song books, S.S. hats, Hitler's personal stationery, an old "potato masher", an actual photo of Himmler under a blanket just after he took poison, a cavalry sword, two war diaries, a Panzer Russian front "frozen meat" medal, plus enough assorted junk to re-equip the Wehrmacht.

Among the most treasured souvenirs is a picture of Madame Declerq astride a tank during the liberation of Brussels. Now Madame Declerq does not tote up to much in the overall story of the gala Bruxellian day. Of immediate interest to you young sweats is the fact that September heralds the twelfth anniversary of this liberation. And for you gamesters of World War I, Madame Declerq should have a story with which you are very familiar.

Those of you who have tasted the "spiritual sweetness" of a city being liberated will appreciate that the section of King's Rules and Regulations covering A.W.O.L. was not always observed. There were many willing hands eager to lead you astray in the most pleasant of fashions. It was my good fortune to be lead from the path of duty by Jean and Georgette Declerq.

There is nothing comparable in civvy street to the emotions of a citizen body being liberated from their oppressors. I stood in the middle of la Place Bruchere in Brussels and gaped while people went raving mad. Old sedate couples cried openly, danced in the streets and drank from the necks of bottles. It was pleasant being kissed by the good ladies, but damned if I could get used to the continental custom of the men likewise hugging me! It was then that Jean and Georgette linked their arms through mine and hauled me off to their home on la Rue Royale as their special captive.

I don't have to tell you blokes how these Belgian mommas can cook. After a three-month diet of dehydrated potatoes, canned cabbage and gasoline-burnt stew, this fiesta nearly broke me out in hives. Seven courses washed down by quarts of different coloured wines and liqueurs made me a stuffed armchair general with the world at his feet.

It was then that Jean decided he would go out and round up some relatives to make up a party. And it was then that Madame Georgette, her lovely face flushed with wine, leaned over and whispered, "Know you a Capitaine Matthews from ze las' war? 'E liv', I tink, in ze place call Toronto."

Now you fellas will have to bear with me because Matthews is not the true name. But as we used to say, "no names, no pack drill". So Matthews it is, sir.

The funny part about all this was that I did know Captain Matthews. I not only knew him; I knew his wife, his kids and his Labrador dog Grouse. As a matter of fact, he was my old boss in civvy street.

But for the life of me I couldn't place the staid and dignified general manager, the president of the Rotary Club, the elder of the church, with Captain Matthews of World War I and Georgette Declerq!

When I cautiously told Madame that I did know of such a party her eyes lit up like Neon dots. Speaking fast and fascinatingly with her eyes, lips and hands, which all Belgian gals do so beautifully, she asked, "An 'ow is zis ranch 'e 'ave? Many cows an 'orses 'e 'ave, eh?"

Ranch? Cows? Horses? I was stumped. She must have sensed my stupid look of bewilderment. Perhaps I had the wrong bloke. It must have been another Captain Matthews. I certainly did not know any rancher by that name . . . especially in Toronto.

"Mais, non," says madame, *"une minute,* I show you." With that she hustles up stairs and digs into her old trunk. In a few shakes she was back fondly displaying a faded brown photo of a dashing young cavalry officer astride his charger. I looked and gaped. There was no doubt about it. It was a youthful face bearing a mustachio, 1916 style, but it was my old boss in civvy street just the same.

Slowly the wheels clicked into place. The mustachios of '16 were no different than the crew cuts of '44. The old familiar Canuck line flashed into mind. "Darling, I love you. Some day I would like to take you back with me to Canada and show you my ranch." Sighs mademoiselle, "Aaaah, thees wild an' romantique Canadiens."

"Mais oui," continues Madame Georgette. "Thees Capitaine Matthews 'e tell me when *la guerre* she begin 'e take all 'is cowboy from 'is ranch in Toronto an' make up wan beeg cavalry regiment, of which 'e is le commandant."

What could I do? You had to be loyal to *the line.* The old *esprit de corps* of Canadians abroad must be maintained. And so I swung into action. Yes, now I remembered. Captain Matthews did have the largest ranch in Toronto but a few years ago he had sold it and retired to "somewhere in California."

As I perjured myself I made a mental note, "Boss, oh boss, if I ever get back to Canada, are you ever going to buy me one large beer! Yes, indeedy."

And so Madame Declerq has her trunk of memories. I wonder how many Dianas, Maries, Rosas and Wilhelminas have theirs? How many of you fellas have yours? Memories that picture, not shrapnel and bursting metal, but sunshine in Bournemouth, or Naples, Calais, Brussels, Amsterdam and Londonderry.

Me! I never told any such fibs like Captain Matthews. Waal, come to think about it, I mind now once I did sort of mention in Ghent about having an interest in a gold mine near Ottawa. But pshaw! that was many years ago. That story will never come to light. Nein? Non? No!

Your Bawth is Ready, Sir!

I was a little shocked recently to get a letter from an old crony who wrote to complain that I was always casting myself in the role of Peck's Bad Boy and seldom highlighted the activities of my "better self."

Said Harry, in a three-page nostalgic throwback: "Smitty, if I didn't know you, I would say that you were the worst old so-and-so that ever came out of the services. But I remember many quiet walks and talks we had in the lanes of Surrey. Why don't you write about the respectable times you had overseas instead of always picturing yourself as the toast of the English pubs?"

To which I say: "Harry, my boy, it could be that you are right. Now that you mention it, we did have some nice, quiet and respectable times in the U.K. But I wonder why these memorable occasions are being consistently buried by the flashbacks of events that were more raucous and physical?"

You know, it is the same when a couple of blokes who haven't seen each other for years meet today in civvy street. They usually sit down for a short beer or a coffee, and the first thing you know they are off to the races about "Remember the time when . . . ?"

Seldom do they talk about the historic day when they went to a church parade at Winchester Cathedral or a conducted tour through Windsor Castle. It invariably develops into a chuckling session about, "Say, you remember the time when that big, red-headed guy was on the carpet for telling the Old Man to . . .", or, "Boy, oh boy! wasn't that some leave we had when we did a pub-crawl in Hammersmith?"

I reckon that it must still be the small boy in all of us that likes to remember the naughty things we did and got away with. Today, if we tried the same tactics, we would cause not only raised eyebrows but virtual isolation by the good respectable citizens in our neighbourhood.

Howsomever, to make you happy, Harry, and those of you who like to hear about the tranquillity of service life, I can think of no more peaceful event than the leave we spent at the home of Lady Bowring.

It was around early '41 when Frenchy Ross and I were teaed and crumpeted at the delightful London home of Lady Frances Ryder. This big-hearted woman had taken it on herself to look after Canadian boys on leave and farm them out to English homes for a spot of rest and change.

Within a few hours we were on a train en route to the snug little hideaway village of Goudhurst in Kent. Alerted by telephone, both Sir George and Lady Bowring were at the station and escorted us back to their comfortable and commodious home.

Ah, this was the life! Beautiful, serene, with the scent of apple blossoms in the air and the war seeming a thousand miles away. We dumped our haversacks in the hall and prepared for a life of ease.

"Oh, by the way," says Lady Bowring, turning towards a tall, black-coated manservant, "this is Symes. He will show you to your room. When you have freshened up, come down to the garden — and we will have a spot of tea together." Righto, pip, pip, and away we go to our four-posted dreamboats. Symes is leading the way, carrying our haversacks like he was afraid they were going to dirty his fingers.

I might have known that this Garden of Eden was too good to be true. Just as Frenchy and I threw our tunics on the beds there was a discreet cough in the background. "I beg your pardon, sir," says Symes, "but will I send down to the station to fetch the rest of your luggage?"

For a moment I was caught flat-footed. Whoever heard of a serviceman on leave having luggage? Hell, all that a fella needed was in that haversack — a tooth brush, a razor, a change of socks, another shirt and enough food coupons for 10 days.

It was then it dawned on me that Symes was the Serpent in this Garden of Eden. That fishy-eyed clam knew ruddy well that we didn't have any more luggage. But he was just slipping the old stiletto into our ribs to remind us that no *real* gentleman ever travelled without luggage.

Howbeit, the day and night went cheerfully, with the Bowrings a charming couple. Surprisingly enough, Sir George had not inherited the mansion but had made his fortune in California from a large orange grove he had established there. He still felt part American and had a soft spot for us Canadians. So we got the royal treatment, including generous measures of his very precious stock of Scotch.

The beds were something to sigh about. You fellas remember what a luxury it was in those days to crawl between fresh linen sheets in a real bed with inner spring mattresses. We, loaded with good food, Madeira wine and a feeling of utter peace and tranquillity, slipped off to sleep.

The next morning, sharp at seven, we awoke with a start as the blackout drapes are thrown back. The sun pours in and there, standing by, is a pleasant-faced maid carrying a tray of steaming hot tea.

Brother, this is the life! I smile across at Frenchy and with an exaggerated air says to him, "Gooood moooorning, dear sergeant, and would you like one lump or two in your tea?" Man, oh man, we were sure riding high! The war was a trillion miles away, and who gave two hoots if we ever saw it again anyhow?

And then I'll be confounded if a shadow didn't cross over the sun and the Serpent was in the room again. "Good morning, sir," says Symes. "I am now running you bath. At what temperature would you like it?"

What temperature would I like it? Hah! that was a beauty for sure. Me, who had spent the last couple of years standing on a cold cement floor under an icy shower, with guys leaving the washroom door wide open!

But Old Baleful Eyes was standing there awaiting further orders. Behind the mask there was a triumphant smirk. He ruddy well knew he had me stumped, and, worse, he knew that I knew it also. He was cutting me down to size in his best gentleman's gentleman fashion. I looked at Frenchy who was looking at me with a hopeless look.

Well, it was either fess up or crawl. But thank the Lord for the native-born ingenuity of the Canadian serviceman. Quick as a flash I says, "At what temperature does Sir George usually have his bath?" Symes, a creature of habit from years of training, unwittingly replies, "Oh, at about 91, sir."

I made a face. "My goodness," says I, "that's far too hot for me. I never have mine above 88 degrees. Please let me know when you have it ready." Poor old Symes. He was licked and he knew it. I could hear him muttering to himself as he left to fetch the temperature gauge.

Symes, old boy, the years have mellowed me now. I no longer despise you. As a matter of fact, I would give anything to see your homely old puss poke its nose in my doorway and say, "At what temperature would you like your bath, sir?"

But I am warning you Symesey, . . . you wouldn't like it. I usually rate sixth on the bath list after the kids have had theirs . . . and you'd have one helluva time getting the old thermo to register at all in the ice cold water they leave behind.

Christmas Overseas

WELL, you refugees from a shubugerie, the Yuletide season is around the clock once again. Gad, it seems that the time flies quicker than a guy snatching his 48-hour pass!

"Whoa, now!" I can hear some jolly airmen and sailors saying. "Slow down, boy; what gives with this word shubugerie?"

If my senile memory serves me correctly, I first came across a real shubugerie around this time of the year in '44. Layers of mist were scattered above the valley that lay between the German positions near the Reichwald forest and the Canadian lines in Holland.

It was customary for those not tied down to frontline positions to do a little social visiting and share a drop of Nelson's Blood with his neighbours. This particular unit happened to be a group of artillery stonkers bedded down snug as a bug in a rug in their shubugeries.

This shubugerie was a log cabin built underground. Again, I need a little refreshing, but you types can correct me if I am wrong. But as I remember it, the walls were made of metal ammo cases filled with earth and sand. The roofs were of three-inch pine heavily topped with soil and so reinforced with canvas or tin that nothing, including rain, could seep through.

This particular one was not only snug but possessed the luxury of electric lights, radios and comfortable beds, with a real carpet on the floor. All this within short shelling distance of the Jerry lines.

The NAAFI Christmas rations had just arrived and it was enough to make your mouth water. The menu read something like this: fruit cup, consomme, roast stuffed pork or canned turkey with vegetables, Christmas pudding with caramel sauce, candies, nuts, cigars, fruit, beer, coffee or tea.

Now this doesn't mean that all the Canadian troops were living it up and doing little else. I can hear some gosh-awful snorts from the Poor Bloody Infantry in the Nijmegen salient who celebrated December 25th by crouching low in their fox-holes and gobbling tins of army stew furtively heated over their tiny paraffin cookers.

However, those who sweated it out on Christmas Day usually were relieved in time to throw their wing-ding on New Year's Day.

Looking back on the scene now through mature eyes, I cannot but help feel proud of the Canadian serviceman. At a time when his own and other lives were in dire jeopardy he still kept his sense of proportion and enjoyed Christmas to the best of his ability.

Take the case of an Ontario regiment that I later visited. Not a rear line echelon but a fighting unit right up there where lead was the accepted currency of the day. Not only did they have cold beer taken from a real refrigerator but the boys were trimming a Christmas tree, complete with electric lights and tinsel.

At the time you didn't ask how a frontline unit within rock-throwing distance of the Hun soil does these things . . . but they did. And if my greasy, well-thumbed diary reads correctly, there are men who, if still alive, will substantiate this — men like Phil Isbister of Hamilton, George Rutherford of Galt and G. W. Durham of Kitchener.

Wherever you went, it was the same old story all over again: Fight hard, play hard. Gad, what stamina these young blokes had!

Not to be outdone in the field of hospitality, the armoured units had their taste of well-being. I remember dropping in on the Governor General's Foot Guards. They not only were planning a bang-up Christmas dinner but several parties as well.

I hesitate to guestimate how many rations went out the back door to purchase "the necessities of life," but the smoker for the men conducted by R.S.M. Harry Venne of Ottawa was a howling success. And just where Sgt. Ronnie Knox, of Kemptville, Ont., scrounged all the material for the decorations is a secret he may never divulge.

And so it was up and down the line. Those behind the lines, while whooping it up, were also busy so that others could be happy.

Take the case of a Motor Ambulance Convoy, R.C.A.S.C. Every spare moment found them in the attic of a Dutch barn. Hammers hammered, saws sawed and files filed as they turned blocks of wood into toy Sherman tanks and Typhoons. Bits of rag and cotton, together with needle and thread, became Orphan Annie dolls. All so some Dutch youngsters would have a jolly Christmas.

In a few short weeks they turned out more than 200 pounds of toys. And that, my friends, is a lot of wood, rags and cotton. The toys ranged from little cars, buses, trucks, tank transporters, ships and airplanes. The chief concern was to keep all hands, including the officers, from spoiling them by too much use before the kiddies' party began!

Officer commanding toys was Sam Hailey of Montreal, and assisting him as designers, decorators and painters, including many others, were Frank Samis of Bowmanville, Ont., and Bill Herchuk of Moose Jaw, Sask.

Of course, no Christmas memory is complete without thoughts of mail and parcels from home. Who can ever forget the well-meaning and welcome parcels from Mom and Aunt Gert, with their home-knitted socks solidly meshed into the fruit cake.

And while others were toiling in their daily fight and their Christmas festivities, let us not forget the Postal Corps, that most cussed and least thanked of all units, which worked around the clock to get the mail to the boys on time.

With groups scattered all over Northwest Europe, one postal unit alone during the Christmas rush handled 2,000 bags of parcels and 45,000 letters daily.

Lest I stray too far in my enthusiasm in telling about the roistering times held by all and sundry, we must never forget those who lay wounded in hospital and for whom the Christmas season could hardly be particularly joyous.

To them, on behalf of those who came through relatively unscathed, all I can say is that we would not cheapen their heroism by pretending that Christmas could be an occasion for celebration for them, but that we remember them with pride and humility.

And then, in a land only a few hundred miles away, but which now seemed thousands, the people of Great Britain were preparing to enjoy their first relaxed Christmas.

The Luftwaffe had been driven from the skies and the Canadians had cleaned up the buzz bomb sights along the Pas de Calais area.

For the first time since 1940 war workers celebrated a four-day holiday. Rations were stepped up and there were to be extras in fats, sugar and sweets.

The president of the Board of Trade announced in stately language that henceforth corsets might be decorated with lace and plush, and might even have a certain amount of elastic inserted in the tops!

And to cap it all, those over 70 years were given a special Christmas present of an extra two ounces of tea. Among the beneficiaries was Winston Churchill who had just passed his 70th birthday on November 30th.

That all seems like many, many years ago, doesn't it, fellas? In a few more days it will be with us again. The kids will romp on the floor, beat their drums and shoot their burp guns. Then will come the moment I always dread as one kid shouts to his pal, "Let's bring this gun over to my pop to fix; he knows all about guns, he used to be in the war."

Then I cringe, remembering all too well the look of pity on our sergeant's face as I lay prone on the ground vainly trying to reassemble the parts of a mystifying Bren gun.

Ah well, chin up, stomach in, shoulders back and other such stout stuff, eh wot?

Getting Even with the Sergeant

IT was one heck of a day as two score and ten of King George's Finest stumped in union o'er the well-trodden Aldershot drill square. Like robots, they clicked along, fighting the desire to unloosen that choking tunic.

Somewhere, seemingly a million miles away, old Iron Jaws kept a-bellering "Left — left — left, right, left. Keep your chin up, you in front! By Gawd, your ruddy mother might love you, but I'm telling you. . ."

"Yak, yak, yak," muttered Slim, out of the corner of his mouth, like only a serviceman can do. "Just wait till this bloody war is over. I'll show that (censored.—Ed.) what a bunch of fives can do!"

"Quiet there in the rear!" roared old Eagle Ears. Just how an R.S.M. could hear a guy muttering one hundred yards away with the wind against him is one of the wartime mysteries never solved. Sometimes I used to think it bordered on magic. Yet the same bloke could be stone deaf when you were only ten feet away and asking for a 48-hour pass.

Several hours afterwards we were sitting on four benches placed around the stove. Most of us were holding our wet, freshly-blancoed webbing equipment in front to dry in the heat of the stove. More equipment hung drying on lines across the hut.

Sitting in this windowless, tunnel-shaped room, with the high double-decker wooden beds crowded along each side, with the fire-light and shadow, the air heavy with heat, there was an air of comfort and camaraderie that I seldom see today.

"Yes-sir," says Slim, "when I get out of this bloody war, the first thing I'm gonna do is walk right up to that sergeant-major and paste him one right on the kisser."

"Me too," chimes in Buck.

The rest nodded sagely as if that was the natural thing for anyone to do.

Y'know, fellas, if I heard that expression once in the last war I heard it a thousand times. And I bet that you alumnae of "40 hommes, 8 chevaux" also heard it in your war. I just wish I had a dollar for every time a serviceman muttered to one side, "Brother, just wait till this war is over. The first thing I'm gonna do is . . . just you wait!

Someday, someplace, I'll meet up with that guy on civvy street and when I do. . .!"

And now the war is over I will wager that not one-tenth of one percent ever carried out their threat to "look that guy up."

Except me. Yes-sir. After seventeen long years I did it. I got even. And, if any zoologist thinks an elephant has a long memory — hah! He should join the services. A serviceman might forgive, but he never forgets.

It all happened a short time ago. Myself and the Little Woman were boarding a bus. I plunked our two tickets in the box and looked for a place to sit. There was none. We were standing in the aisle when the driver barked, "Step to the rear of the bus, please!"

That voice. It shocked me. There could be none other. I looked. Sure enough, it was *him*. No, I didn't see a fat, multi-jowled man with a grizzly mustache. It wasn't a paunchy driver perched on a high seat. It was a big, fierce-mustached man with a scowl on his face and three stripes on his arm.

It wasn't the bus I was standing in. It was a huge bull-pen at the Exhibition Grounds in Toronto. It wasn't a pad of transfers the driver had in his hand, but a silver-headed swagger cane. He wasn't saying, "Step to the rear of the bus, please." Instead, he was roaring, "You there, on the double and haul the lead out!"

There was no doubt about it. The bus driver was ex-Sergeant Sweeney. Brother, he was a real mean 'un, that I could never forget.

Now believe me fellas, I have been chewed out by plenty since Sweeney did his soul-searing job on me. And, being no stranger to such things as A.W.L. a day or so, plus a nodding acquaintance with guardhouses from Debert to Aldershot, I hold no grudge for the chewings out I got from sergeants, adjutants, C.O.'s and, once, a real live brigadier. But this Sweeney, he was real mean and dirty.

It was back in '40 and I was standing for roll-call in the bull-pen at the Ex. in Toronto. Clutched as my most precious possession was my docket entrusted to me by the recruiting officer. We stood there in our civvies, half-quaking inside at this new and terrifying form of life. Alert, and as anxious to please as a young Labrador puppy.

You remember those days? When a guy with two stripes on his arm was a real big shot. And a three striper — well, he was just about King Kong himself. They pushed you around with the scorn of a Genghis Khan and you scampered and hustled to get into line. And the biggest part of you was your feet.

Well, sir, as I said, I was standing with the group and Sweeney, he was bellering off names. When your name was called you scampered to a chosen spot and you knew that at least you belonged to either "A" or "B" Company.

Came the end of the roll-call. Sweeney snaps his book shut and was about to yell, "Corporal, take over!" And then he looks . . . and he looks again. And there, standing alone in the centre of this high bull-pen, was lowly little R65150, Smith, D. W.

"What the hell are you doing there?" he roars.

I quaked. I quivered. And two hundred pairs of eyeballs swung towards the lone, shaking figure.

"Please, sir," says I, "you didn't call my name."

Oh, that *was* the wrong thing to say. Never, never, never accuse a senior man of being in the wrong. Sweeney flushed right up to the lobes of his dangling ears. He just stood there, his lips rolling back from his teeth.

"And what," says he in a deadly, quiet voice, "did you say your name was?" I told him. He gives his book a hurried run down, and then he lets blast. Oh, the narsty things that man said! Says he, winding up, "And furthermore, I distinctly remember calling your name."

Why is it that mothers give their sons parting advice? My mother, bless her, had always said, "Son, if you are in the right, and you know that you are right, then stick to your guns."

Don't laugh fellas. I took her sage advice. Says I, almost boldly, "But you did NOT, sir."

And then the ruddy roof fell in.

For thirty long miserable days I sweated it out. Sweeney took to me like a sore bear with a hate against the world. And I was his particular world. Not a step did I take but it was wrong. My bunk was made and re-made. My polished boots to him were filthy things. When the company was let out to attend an I.O.D.E. party, I was detailed for fatigues. He never eased up once. He wasn't trying to make a soldier out of me. He was just being plain mean and dirty.

That was seventeen years ago. Now we are back in the bus again and that voice barks out, "Step to the rear of the bus, please!" Only to me that voice wasn't a bus driver, it was a mean 'un bellering at me with bared teeth.

The crowd moves dutifully back, but I hold firm. I'm three steps away from Sweeney.

The Little Woman is tugging on my sleeve. "Come on," she whispers, "everybody is looking at you."

So is Sweeney. And I'm looking right back at him. The blood again, as in days of yore, mounts to the lobes of his dangling ears as he rebellers, "Will you step to the rear of the bus!"

The white shows through my knuckles as I clutch the handle of the seat alongside. But I don't budge an inch.

I look Sweeney right in the eye, but he doesn't recognize me. Five seconds later he breaks off the clash. With a grunt and a mutter he throws his gear-shift savagely into low and away we go.

Twenty-minutes later we are off the bus and walking close to home when the Little Woman says, "Whatever got into you in that bus? I thought you and that bus driver were going to come to blows."

It was then that the humour of it all struck me. Poor old Sweeney. Suddenly I wasn't mad at him any more. But how do you go about explaining that to a civilian?

You fellas will understand, I know.

Those Saturday Morning Parades

ONE of the happiest thoughts that I had on discharge was, "Thank the Lord, now there will be no more compulsory parades." Hah! What a naive character I was. Since then I have attended more compulsory parades than a bloke with an eight-page crime sheet.

Every Saturday morning the Little Woman puts on her shopping best, opens the barrack door and in a firm voice says, "No. 1 platoon will advance in column of route, B Section leading!" Then out troop the Smith family, board the convoy and head for the establishment boasting the largest bargain advertisement in last night's paper.

I watch them file by. "Gad, sir," I say to myself, "if this keeps up I will have enough to complete a section. I wonder how much Ottawa would pay a fella if he offered a section complete, all trained and in marching order? Could be they might make me a ruddy colonel! I have seen red tabs hooked on for less."

Anyhow, as I said, this compulsory parade business is something that should be taken up at the next Dominion Convention. It is not too late to assert our rights. There was nothing in the recruiting papers at the church that said we had to attend Saturday morning parades. Comrades, unite! Let us strike a blow for freedom! Let us tell these culinary R.S.M.'s that we protest! The first comrade that does so successfully, please write and tell me how he did it and . . . got away with it. I will then send him the HUSBANDS' VOLUNTEER LIBERATION MEDAL, struck especially for the occasion.

Well, fellas, to continue in bondage. B Section arrived at rendezvous at exactly ten hundred hours. Appropriately it was an Army and Navy store. The R.S.M. said there would be a 30-minute break but to stand by for further movement orders. The "recruits" highballed it for the toy-gun department, the R.S.M. swooped into the Q.M. stores marked "Specials," and me — acting corporal, unpaid, Smith — was left alone in a sea of human tanks manoeuvring for position.

Eventually this tidal wave carried me along and cast me to one side on a barren coast marked "War Surplus Supplies." Y'know, fellas, I had the pleasantest 30 minutes that I had spent in years. There I was, alone among the glories of the past. I laissez-faired about in a nostalgic Utopia. Here were things to delight an old sweat's memory. Cast-offs and misfits though they might be, I fingered each article fondly as I escaped to a bygone yesterday.

Army tunics, some with their flashes intact. I picked up one still proudly boasting the red flash of the P.P.C.L.I. A little tag flaunted the price — $2.59. What price glory? Who had worn this tunic? Was it from the belongings of some valiant soul now resting in Holland? Or was its owner today one of the wooden faces blending in with the sameness of the five o'clock bus.

Alongside, a pile of air force tunics lay in disarray. Old they were, with worn grey shodding through the blue. A bright spot stood on one sleeve where a patch had once been sown. What patch had been there? Had it been an L.A.C. badge? The sparks of a W.A.G.? Who had so proudly worn it? Who had stood in front of a mirror many times to see how that badge of honour showed? Who, each time his photograph was taken, had carefully edged that right arm forward so the badge would be prominently displayed for the folks back home? Who?

Along the bins two youths were excitedly holding up some army haversacks. "Just the thing to put the birds in and only 39 cents. I'm getting two," says one callow 'teener. I picked up a rumpled haversack. Inside the flap a name was printed with an indelible pencil. Boldly the name stood out. "K 543879 — R. STOREY". Well, well, Number K 543879; little did you dream years ago when you carefully wetted your purple pencil that your haversack would wind up duck hunting.

Perhaps the most cussed and maligned character in the last war was the poor cook. As graceless gourmets filed past his stew pots with their mess-tins outstretched, he heard himself called many peculiar names. Few of them were flattering. I know. Many's the time I gave them the filthy look treatment as some nameless goulash was slobbered into my tin. "Call that food?" — "Which side you guys fighting on?" — "How much the Jerries paying you?" — "Just to think we used to feed this guck to the pigs back home." And so on.

But now I feel different towards the poor cooks. I take it all back, matey. I never knew what you had to put up with. It is a wonder to me you didn't all end up in a head doctor's arms.

There on the shelf in this store was a large tin marked "Dehydrated Cabbage. Eight pounds net, $1.98." I was sorely tempted to buy a tin just for old times' sake. But the next line stopped me. "Each pound makes 48 to 68 servings." I did a quick recap. That meant there was enough cabbage in that tin to feed 544 men. If I brought it home, the Smith family would be eating dehydrated cabbage until they were old enough to vote.

No, I would never get away with it. Blimey, tho'. Those poor cook critturs. Imagine trying to make a tasty dish out of rations like that!

Why shoot the cook? He should have got a medal for having to face the stuff day in and day out.

The bins were littered with castoffs. Steel helmets, 98 cents. Nothing looks so useless as a tin helmet in civvy street. I picked one up. About the only use it would be at home would be for a flower pot. And yet a few short years ago it was one of a soldier's most precious possessions.

We were lucky in the last war. We did not have to use our gas masks. I rummaged through a pile of them labelled "Only .49 cents". What in blazes could a fella do with a gas mask in civvy street? Kids were trying them on. "I'm a spaceman," yells one. "Aw, come on," yells another, "they cost too much anyway. Let's go and get a real mask."

Poor, blighted gas mask. Nobody wants you at even 49 cents. Nobody really wanted you in the last war. Whenever gas drill was called and men had to haul the rubber bands over their heads, they groaned aloud. And yet, I mused, what wouldn't the boys at Ypres have given for the caress of their ugly protection. What price 49 cents?

Thirty minutes later I had more caboodle in my arms than a quartermaster on clothing parade. Yes sir, I was loaded down with haversacks, woollen navy sweaters, heavy socks, life belts, ammunition pouches and water bottles.

About then the R.S.M. and Section B hove into view. "Yikes!" she yelled and then slowly moaned, "Oh, no, no, no! We should never have left him alone in here."

But by that time, fellas, she was a little too late. Pride of rank had returned. Up came the chins, back went the shoulders, out went the chest and in came the stomach. With a bark in my voice I growled, "That will be enough! Enough, do you hear? All aboard for home!"

Fellas it was wonderful. Not once did anyone open a lip. We passed two restaurants without one howl of "We wanna treat". And when we arrived home there was an almost respectful wariness.

Now, then, I says to myself is the time to strike my HUSBANDS' VOLUNTEER LIBERATION MEDAL. I think that it will portray a father astride a prancing white charger. Beneath him are a woman and several angelic children all gazing fondly upwards. Underneath will be inscribed that famous motto taken from the ancient French heraldry, *"Vive le poppa, il est le boss."*

I will forward such medal upon application to any veteran who can qualify. All he has to do is to live up to this motto. But he must have an affidavit to this effect signed by his wife and . . . countersigned by his mother-in-law.

Veterans of Canada unite! *"Vive le poppa, il est le boss!"*

Caen – July 1944

THE front door was wide open, the windows were open, the curtains were flapping in the breeze and the Little Woman was saying things that no self-respecting sergeant-major would utter.

"When," says she, "are you going to get off your fat you-know-what and put some screen doors up for us? We are sick and tired of trying to eat good food spoiled by swarming flies."

"Aw," says I, "what t'heck are a few flies. Why, when I was in . . ."

"Yeah," chimed in the kids, "when you were in Normandy the flies were big as bumblebees and they came down in clouds. Pop, you always start that routine, but please, please, get us some screens."

Gad, y'know fellas, it gets tougher every year for an Old Sweat to get away with anything. Nothing's sacred anymore, not even tales of yesteryear.

That is why I like writing for you blokes; here at least I have a sympathetic ear. You guys know why a few flies in the house never bother me. Anyone who was in Normandy remembers them vividly.

Flies . . . Man! with the stultifying heat and the rotting carcasses of thousands of cows along the hedgerows, the big blue bottle bloated blimps lived with you night and day. When you woke up it wasn't because there was a fly on your twitching face; it was a swarming cluster thick as a bunch of grapes.

Along about the same time that I was getting keel-hauled for not protecting the youth of today from the death-dealing potentials of house flies, the TV set came on with a doozer of a program.

I don't know how many of you saw the one-hour extravaganza about D-Day, but this year's show was a real lulu. A great deal of it was American, but there was enough of ours in it to make a real thriller.

Like a kid away from home too long I was spellbound when shots of the Caen of today flashed on the screen.

What I was looking for and hoping to see, I really don't know. But there was a new and modern city. A community of well laid-out houses, smartly sophisticated stores and towering office buildings. It left me with mingled feelings. And then I realized that I was secretly looking for something I would never see again. In true essence I was an old man chasing dreams.

But who among us that have been there can ever forget the Caen that we first saw? The shattered, battered city that rocked under 2,000 tons of Air Force bombs on D-Day alone. And to complete the macabre picture, another large-scale blasting occurred on July 18 when 1,000 Lancasters and Halifaxes smothered the area with thousands of bombs and incendiaries.

The smoke had not cleared away when 1,500 Fortresses and Liberators of the American 8th Air Force rained down more death and destruction. Then, to make doubly certain, 600 American mediums beat up what was left with fragmentation bombs.

Not to be outdone thousands of Allied artillery pieces formed a ten-mile semi-circle around Caen and fired night and day without letup. You would swear that nothing could live or stand under that continuous onslaught.

Yet, before the smoke had rolled away, hundreds of British tanks rolling along were stopped in their tracks by German guns that had been left untouched. Village after village in the Caen area was heavily defended and had its compliment of guns. It takes a lot of dying to kill a city.

In the TV shots they showed a spanking new water reservoir. It was here in front of the TV that the old man really got chasing dreams.

You blokes remember when Caen was first taken over. The water supply was shot and all that remained were a few village troughs and the dirtied waters of the Orne.

This seemed fine at first until the Caenites came back from their caves and started to use them also. With perfect innocence they allowed their horses, their cows and their dogs to drink from the same troughs. It didn't faze them one iota.

What with the flies and the slimed-up waters, the hospitals back near Bayeaux were soon treating more dysentery than gun shot cases.

Then the Civil Affairs blokes took over. They commandeered a water works, patched up a few pumps, installed a generator, a purifying system and put a Frenchman named Charles in charge.

Charles was right proud of his job, which consisted only of watching the machinery to see that nothing went wrong. However, one evening Charles saw to his horror either the pumps go haywire or the water main break and the place became flooded. In case of such an emergency all Charles had to do was to pull a switch and shut off a few valves.

However, the sight of all that water flooding around him was too much for Charles and he fled into the night, reporting the emergency to no one. Hours and thousands of gallons later they went searching for Charles. They found him at home. A terrified wife said he was in his bedroom a sick man.

It was there they found poor Charles who, finding his problems too much to bear, had plunged into bed, boots and all on, and hauled the covers over his head.

The fading scenes of D-Day passed from the TV screen and the family, sensing that the old man was again back in the land of the living, started to chorus:

"Hey, pop, when ARE you going to put up the screens?"

"Screens, screens, hell," I snarled. "Why, when I was in Normandy you got tired of swatting the flies off your bread until you were ready to take a bite. And then you didn't know which was flies and which was black currants. What's more, you didn't give a damn."

There was a shocked silence.

"Out, out, out!" they yelped in indignant chorus at this uncouth old soldier, who forthwith sneaked out — the backway to commune with his ever-loving and understanding hound-dog who didn't seem to mind the flies one bit.

When Smitty came Marching Home

IF anyone was to ask me what were my two most exciting days in the services I would list them as follows:

(a) The day I was sworn in.

(b) The day I got my discharge.

Nobody but the dullest clod could refrain from a spine-tingling thrill as you stood in front of the recruiting officer, raised your right hand, and took the oath of allegiance.

From that point on life took on an entirely new meaning.

The first night in barracks, the strange sounds.

The proper bahstud of a corporal who treated you like you were something under a microscope.

The ill-fitting uniform, with its narrow-bottom trousers, the large, black boots, the narrow wedge-cap which kept falling over your ear.

As you strolled down Main Street for the first time in uniform you were certain that everybody, but everybody in town, was staring especially at you.

You peeked self-consciously in store windows to see how you looked, and you blushed like hell when you realized that the guy you had just saluted was only the doorman outside the hotel.

I've had many self-conscious moments in my chequered career, but nothing to compare with my first few weeks in uniform.

However, the thrill to surpass all thrills was the time five years later when you knew that someday now, any day perhaps, your number would come up and you would go home.

Back to civvie street! Boy, what you weren't going to do! The very first thing would be to go to the poshest restaurant in town with your special girl friend and order the biggest, the juiciest and the most succulent steak in the house — and hang the expense.

Then, if he ever crossed your path, you were going to go up to that particular N.C.O., or that s.o.b. of an officer, and were you ever going to give that bloke a piece of your mind! And, if he uttered one peep — just one small bleat — you'd poke him right on the snoot.

Yes-siree, that's just what you were going to do.

I know there was one particular R.S.M. for whom I had a fate all planned out. I wasn't even going to make with the small talk. I was just going to let him have it . . . hard.

Several years after discharge I ran into him at a Legion hall. I was having a few beers. This guy walks in. He spots me and I spot him. I spring from my seat. He strides towards me.

"Smitty!" he cries.

"Sa'hunt-major, you old son of a gun!" I yell.

Three minutes later we are downing beer like thirsty camels, with arms around each other's shoulders.

Yep, I sure kept my long-promised vow — hah! I wonder how many of you fellas did likewise?

However, I guess that's all water under the bridge now. Except at one time it was all very real with you.

Little things like points. How many of them did you have? Surely with 200 points they would be posting your name any day now for repatriation. And yet the call did not come.

Meantime, you heard through the most reliable source, Daily Routine Rumours, that some jokers with only 78 points were on their way home. You cussed the services and all those in authority for a bunch of lazy, sloppy, indifferent plugs. Guys who didn't give a damn as long as they filled their quota with any odds and sods nearby.

You stewed in the bunkhouse and wrote long, promising notes home until there wasn't anything left to write anymore.

You went on leave. One final more fling at the Big Town. But it wasn't the same. There was a gnawing restlessness to get the hell out of there and get home. What you were going home to you weren't quite certain. But home was home and that was the one place in the world you wanted to go to most.

Then came the big moment. Your name came up. You were on your way to a repat depot.

You never in all your life saw a guy fling stuff so fast into a duffle bag. Never did you salute so smartly as when you reported to the orderly room, apprehensive lest by some freak of fate any slip or misconduct on your part would take you off the roster.

Feverishly you gave excess baggage away to buddies who called you "lucky dog." Furtively you tucked that German Luger way down between a pair of heavy socks.

You still couldn't believe your luck. And it was only when the 60 hundredweight began pulling away from the camp and you waved goodbye from the tailboard that it finally dawned on you that you were really on your way. Or at least the first step of many steps to come had been taken.

You crossed the Channel and again you bunked down somewhere near Farnham. Brightly you went to the orderly room with that hopeful question on your lips, "When do I sail?"

"Watch for your name on the notice board," drones a sadly disillusioned corporal who knows *he* is frozen and couldn't care less when *you* got home.

And so day in and day out you watch that board. Drafts leave and still your name never appears.

By this time you have played all the cribbage you can stand, drunk all the nut-brown ale that the NAAFI can supply, said farewell to your English friends, and stared at the pictures in your wallet with a yearning out of this world.

And still your name doesn't come up. The hours, the days and even the weeks go by. Yet back in Amsterdam they had given you three hours to pack and hurry-hurry-hurry.

Then the lowness sets in. Your morale droops lower than a mongrel's tail. You live and breathe ship movements. Rumours fly around, despondent rumours, and you are fair game for them all.

Latest on the rumour rounds is the *Lizzie*. The *Lizzie* has been taken off and sent to the Pacific . . . the *Empress of Scotland* was in dry dock and wouldn't be off for a month . . . civilians were travelling ahead of troops . . . low-pointers were going home and high-pointers were frozen, etc., etc.

You ran hot and cold with each eagerly devoured rumour until fact no longer existed and fiction ruled the day. There was no fact in your life for the simple reason the authorities never told you any facts.

Then came the fateful day when you saw your name on the board. You stared at it, fascinated. And you looked, and looked, and looked, and prayed that there was no mistake.

There was no mistake. For once in its ruddy life the Army had done something right. And you didn't mind the eight-tiered bunks in the troopship's hold. You would have slept on coal sacks in a corner if it meant getting across that ocean . . . and home.

Then came the distant shoreline of Halifax. And if you didn't actually get down and kiss the dock, you did so in your mind.

No longer did the fussing, officious little tin-pots annoy you as they herded you aboard the train. No longer did you fret and fume as you waited in the long dining room queue.

No more did you swear as the old sway-backs of racked-out troop trains roared around the curves, tossing you helter-skelter in your sleeper. For the sweetest music in the world was that rackety-tackety-tack as the wheels ground over the rails, and each whoooo, whoooo of the engine's whistle brought you that much closer to home.

Then your train puffed into the hometown station. The bands were playing, the flags were flapping, the crowds were cheering and your heart was pounding, but you paid no heed. Somewhere, but somewhere, in that sea of faces were the ones you loved.

And then you saw them — mom, dad and the girl of your dreams. This indeed was home! The end of a road. More roads would come — but none would ever be the same.

Gongs and Ribbons

RUMMAGING around the old duffle-bag the other day I dragged out my set of medals. Tarnished they were, with the ribbons fading into mediocre dullness. I gazed at the ribbons and thought to myself how proud of them we once were. Even the lowly Volunteer Service Medal which we wore with singular pride had a background of humour attached to it. As all of us overseas at the time were volunteers, it meant that everybody wore one and so, in patronizing fashion, we tagged it the Spam Medal.

Yet the Spam Medal meant something at the time. Our British cousins had nothing to sport and amid the glory of the Yankee fruit salad you couldn't differentiate between medals for valour and those for bird-watching. And so the Spam Medal with its maple leaf clasp was to us a symbol of distinction.

Those were days when medals meant something. An individual wore them with pride. In an era when physical valour was the complete yardstick of manliness we secretly admired the man behind the ribbons.

It was the R.A.F. lads who first sported their gongs. Royal Air Force types spotted in pubs wearing the D.S.O., D.F.C., or D.F.M. certainly commanded great respect. And rightly so.

The others who were the envy of all ambitious young sprouts were the Old Sweats of the First World War. A man could have obvious personal limitations but the wearing of his ribbons automatically upped him a notch in any company.

I suppose the one soldier who caused the most commotion overseas was a "re-tread" stationed at C.M.H.Q. in London. He was Sergeant-Major Thomas James. He had been a commissioned officer in the First War and came out of it an Acting Colonel with a whack of D.S.O.'s, M.C.'s, M.I.D.'s and various Indian, Persian and Mespot campaign ribbons — in short, an unusual lot of fruit salad.

Somehow or other he managed to re-enlist in 1939, passed his physical and wangled his way overseas as an N.C.O. Too old for field duty, they gave him a desk job at C.M.H.Q. He did fine at his work, but his biggest terror was walking anywhere along the Strand or at a railway station. There the Military Police, ever conscious of spies infiltrating our ranks, zealously picked up anyone in uniform not conforming to all the accepted standards of dress.

And so whenever they spotted the Old Sweat marching along with his D.S.O. and M.C. ribbons, etc., etc., and he not even a commissioned officer, they promptly said, "Hah, a spy!" and lugged him into Intelligence for questioning.

The poor bloke became so harassed by ambitious M.P.'s that the C.M.H.Q. brass finally gave him an official letter to show that "he was a good, honest volunteer and not a German agent trying to imitate a Canadian soldier."

As I said before, medals in those days were the yardsticks of a man. There was little appreciation of "fineness of the mind". A man could be a proper S.O.B., but if he wore a medal of valour the general consensus was, "Well, the buzzer has got many failings but you have to hand it down to the guy, he must have something on the ball." Or, as Robbie Burns would put it, "A man's a man for a' that."

I think that the greatest shot in the arm for the morale of the Canadian troops was the news that one of their own had been decorated for heroism. D.S.O.'s, M.C.'s, D.F.C.'s, M.M.'s and D.C.M.'s were all accorded their proper respect. But towering, way and beyond them was the coveted and much worshipped Victoria Cross. Here was the symbol, the highest accolade of man's bravery, the ribbon that held the awe of all from Field-Marshal and Private.

I remember what a thrill we got in Normandy when it was announced that Major David Currie of the South Alberta Regiment, the 29th Recce, was awarded the V.C. for his part in the action at St. Lambert-sur-Dives which cut the Chambois-Trun escape route for the German Seventh Army trapped in the Falaise pocket.

Weary and dog-tired as everyone was at that time, the news electrified all ranks. It was like a member of your family had become a national hero and you somehow a part of it.

Then, of course, I can never forget Major Currie's remarks when he was asked by the press how it felt being a V.C. winner. "Well," says he, "I am a little worried about how my wife Isabel will take it. She'll be mad at me, I know. I told her that when I came over here I was going to keep my head down . . . way down."

Around about September '44 we had hurriedly moved the *Maple Leaf* up from Caen and set up shop in the splendid quarters of *Le Soir* in Brussels. After the rubble of *La Presse Caenaisse* this was a newspaperman's dream.

I got to know most of the Belgian newspapermen pretty well. But the one who really intrigued me was their newly appointed war correspondent. One day he was in civvies and the next he appeared decked out in the snazziest dress uniform you ever saw. His high boots polished and shone, his breecks were of the finest material and his tailored tunic fitted him like Betty Grable's dresses. But the thing that really held my awe was the three rows of ribbons that he sported on his left chest.

I had known the bloke for a week before when he wore civvies. He was the last to impress you as a "fighting fool." But by this time I had seen enough real men to shatter my pre-war illusions that all heroes were big, rough, bluff and tough. And so I gave the guy full marks and respect for his rows of medals.

However, one night I queried my good Bruxellian friend Olivier Delville. "How come?" I says. "You haven't had an army in action since '40 and yet this character wears all those gongs?"

Forthwith Delville just about choked on his cognac and exploded into prolonged spasms of laughter. Finally his apoplexy disappeared and, wiping the tears away from his eyes, he said, "Those medals! Hell, I've got eight or ten of them at home myself! You want a medal? O.K., leave it to me. I'll see that you get one."

Sure enough, about a month later I got a call from Delville. "Smitty," says he. "There is to be a press conference at one of the embassies this afternoon. I would like you to come along with me."

Like a good soldier and newspaperman I couldn't very well turn down an offer of free eats plus free drinks, so I accepted.

It was one of those posh affairs thrown by a small South American embassy. The ambassador was all rigged out in his tails and striped pants with a big ribbon around his neck and more miniatures on his chest than Montgomery.

Came the end of his speech and up steps a flunkey with a tray having a blue velvet base. Gleaming on the velvet were a dozen silver crosses with ribbons of orange, black and red. Solemnly as my name was called I stepped forward, the ambassador gives me a hug, a slushy peck on each cheek and pins the medal on my tunic.

I staggered out of there glass-eyed in disbelief. "What gives? What in blazes gives?" I gasped to Delville.

"That, my friend," says he, "is an old embassy custom over here. Everytime they have an official function the ambassador passes out those medals as an act of good will. Stick around with me, boy, and I'll make you a hero in nine weeks!"

I still have that glamour medal, though it, too, has become tarnished and faded. However, it had its days of glory. I wore the ribbon on my leave back to the U.K. It was great to watch the blokes at the pubs eyeing it, at first curiously and then, unable to restrain themselves, sidling up to me and query, "I say, old boy; pardon the intrusion, but would you mind telling me what that ribbon represents?"

"Oh that," says I, casually looking down at the glamorous thing beside my lowly Spam ribbon, "is something I picked up in a South American show."

"Oh," say they, vaguely, and return to their beer more mystified than ever.

Yup, some of it was fun.

Newfie Screech is Powerful Stuff!

PLUNK in the middle of a deep leather chair in a Newfie Legion branch I watched the mellow glow of the dying sun basking on the potentest hair-restorer of the Seven Seas.

I have watched with glee as a Johnnie-Come-Lately gasped on his first slug of Calvados. The horrors of a vino victim has made me close my eyes in sympathetic meditation. But the greatest pleasure in life is to watch a "Mainlander's" eyeballs pop when he downs his first Screech neat.

Unblemished by Confederation issues, the Newfie screech still retains its proof plus strength in dynamic force, enough to shade Kickapoo Juice in the mothers' milk class.

A Saturday night in a typical Legion hut. By the wall a foursome were fiercely battling for that precious "double one". In a far corner a quartette were whooping it up as both needed a vital two points to peg out.

With a faraway look an ex-bombardier was tinkling the ivories and strumming up nostalgic memories with " 'Till the Lights of London Shine Again".

Dead around me the Saturday night kibitzers were stringing little stories of their battles in Normandy and large, lengthy pantomimed orations on their victories in Paris.

The bloodless battle of Confederation will never die in memory. Bitter opponents of the amalgamation still exist.

Strongest anti-Confederate is Danny. When Churchill was a boy Danny was toting a gun. And he has been shooting one in every war since. By the looks of him, with his grizzled face and fierce mustache, he seems to be a hundred years old.

The fact remains that when it comes to shooting guns Danny knows his powder. He skirmished with the Fuzzy Wuzzies, guerillaed against the Boers, bled with the decimated Royal Newfoundlanders at Beaumont Hamel, and handled a carbine in the Veterans' Guard in the last show.

"Confederation," snorted Danny. "Hell! iffen it weren't for us Newfoundlanders, all them bloody Mainlanders would be Yanks today."

The Oldtimer was really shootin' the breeze. I reckoned it was the Screech talking and ignored his statement.

"Don't believe me, huh?" leered the four times recipient of the King's Shilling.

"Why, you young punks don't know nothin', nothin' at all about your history. My great grandfather was making history before you book-learners ever though about it. Confederation is it you're talkin' about? Hell, there weren't no Canada today iffen it weren't for a bunch of fightin' Newfoundlanders."

The Oldtimer was in dead earnest. Any guy that's pulled a trigger in four shows should know his way around. So I gave with, "How come, Danny, what's the story behind the story?"

"Well," said the Oldtimer. "Don't mind iffen I do," as he acknowledged the two fingers of Screech placed before him.

"You guys thought you was hard done by when you had to go overseas in a big troopship. Way back in the seventeen hundreds my great-grandfather came right smack across from Devon in a 10-ton schooner. He never had no compass to steer him by, just the sun and a beaten path across the Atlantic for hundreds of years by his folks."

Here he paused, reinforced himself with one fingerful and pounded the table, "Why, hell's bells, iffen it weren't for my kinfolk and the Newfie fishermen there wouldn't be no British Empire at no time at all."

I eyed the screech with open-eyed admiration. It sure could draw on the longbow in mortals. With Dutch courage from its glow I scoffed at the Oldtimer.

"Crazy, am I?" roared the thoroughly aroused old warrior. "Let me tell you young nine-day wonders a few facts of life."

"When the Spaniards come across the Atlantic with their invincible Armada to lick the tarnation out of the English fleet, who was it what whomped them in the keels? It were the little boats of Sir Francis Drake what did it.

"And where did Drake get his men to man the small boats? Why, from the Banks of Newfoundland, of course. Yes sir, they sailed rings around them big galleons, and from that day on the British Empire grew."

Blast me for a NAAFI cowboy! The Oldtimer really had something there. I needled him on.

Downing the second finger he brushed his fierce mustache and rambled on.

"Never heard of the Royal Emigrants, I suppose? Nope, didn't figure them fancy school books had much to learn you. Back in 1775 my great-grandfather was doing his chores when a red-coat named Captain Colin Campbell came high-tailing it down to Newfie. In a right powerful hurry he was. The Americans was raising hell all over the Continent. Their army was hugging the French lassies in Montreal and gobbling up the old man's pea soup. In a short time they would have Quebec, and all Canada would be theirs.

"This Captain Campbell he told the story to my folk and they quit their fishin' and formed the Royal Emigrants. More than 300 Newfoundlanders made up the small group of 1,800 men that was defending the last main British garrison in Canada.

"The Americans came storming in on a 31st December aimin' to fill their mess-kits in the fort for New Year's Day. They was doin' all right until they ran smack into the Royal Emigrants. The boys upped and socked 'em good and hard, killed their General Montgomery and saved Canada."

By that time the whole Legion group was around. Danny was the M.C. of the evening.

"Who knows anything about the Royal Newfoundland Fencibles?" he queried. The ignorant stood dumbly about.

"Didn't reckon any of you, with your blabbermouth talk about Confederation, did," he snorted.

"The second time them Americans comes gallupin' up into Canada they had the troops on the run again. Long about 1812 the Old Fencibles moved up to Halifax and then on to defend Fort Erie and Fort York. Whomped them Americans again, they did. When they finished up in 1815 they came home fishin'.

"Confederation! Hell, we paid our price of admission years and years ago. We got a bigger stake in that country than any bonus payments will ever make up for . . . Leff me bide now; the rattlin' of your brains disturbs me thoughts."

The Legion hall was quiet. The picture of Field-Marshal Haig beneath the Jack looked down in understanding tranquillity.

The Padre, a Real Man

THE congregation were slowly filing out of the village church. The good clergyman was smiling and shaking hands at the door. I was next in line. "Nice sermon, padre," I says. He looked and he jumped, "Smitty, my boy, you old so-and-so." He collected himself rapidly and, in the quick aside of an old soldier, said, "I'll see you later." He then continued on with commiserations about the next lady's ailments.

In the cool of the eve and safely buried in his study we reminisced for hours as only old sweats can do.

If you think that you guys had a tough job getting rehabilitated, you should be a padre to really have a conversion job. From the front line life of a rootin', tootin' outfit to the genteel life of a village clergyman — man, you have to do some fast rehabilitating.

From a life where you got the best results by speaking straight from the shoulder to guys who could take it, to a congregation that like their truths sugar-coated, was a big change. The padre did it, as must have hundreds of others. I wonder if any failed? I wonder how many bucked the well known order, didn't compromise and had a really tough time of it?

As I said, we got to talking about old times. Said he, "You remember Major Johnston of the 5th Div?" I opined that I remembered the padre from Brantford very well. His name brought to memory a hearty, jovial man with a good appetite for life in all its healthy forms.

I remembered the time when "Judge" George Morrison, of Sydney, and another chap and I were part of an advance party to East Anglia. Enroute to Cockley Cley in Norfolk we visited Cambridge. After going through King's and Trinity Colleges we spent a pleasant hour punting on the Cam.

It was late and we had to move along. It was also Sunday. Passing a church we were greeted by an elderly clergyman. He took hold of our arms and tried to lead us into the church for the service. We protested that it was raining and we had to push along. The old clergyman shook his head, "Come along now. I know you Canadians, you have to be coaxed." Then, turning, he innocently added, "And besides, Major, you look as if a bit of religion might help you."

The major was Padre Johnston. We ribbed him about it for months. I hope he sees this story and gets the same kick out of it that we always did.

Civilians who think that the troops were godless, hell-raising creatures should ask any padre. He will tell you differently. He will tell you that most of this attitude was on the surface, that underneath ran a deep religious faith that can only be experienced by men who had a daily rendezvous with death.

The troops had a great affection for their padres. Few, and none that I know of, ever let them down.

When the 5th Div. was settled down near West Hoathly and Forest Row in Sussex in 1943, the R.C. boys had a great love for an elderly sister in the nearby Notre Dame Convent.

Every Sunday morning she would line up "her boys" and march them to Mass. She gave her orders expertly and the parade was the most orderly on record. One Sunday morning she was singled out and presented with a sergeant-major's brass badge. It was solemnly pinned on the left sleeve of her black habit. Thereafter she was affectionately called "Sergeant-Major" — and the only one in the Canadian Army to be saluted by all ranks. I wonder if Father Jim McIsaac of Winnipeg remembers this occasion?

On the Continent, under fire, the padres did a wonderful job. Outside of the frontline heroics of comforting wounded and dying men while under fire, they performed other tasks that took real stomach. Those who remember the burning hot days of July and August in Normandy will agree that fingerprinting and recording decomposed corpses was a job that called for intestinal fortitude of the highest order.

Whenever possible the padres arranged a service. Often the Word of God was preached within striking distance of the enemy lines. If a guy was not a devout convert you seldom heard any snide off-side remarks as you oftimes do in civvy street. A man's religion was his own business and he was respected for his belief.

I will never forget how impressed I was in Germany when Rabbi Samuel Cass of Montreal held an outdoor service. The solemn reciting of the Shema Yisroel in a land where Jews had been persecuted for years was a triumph for God-fearing people. The work that Rabbi Cass did in the misery, filth and squalor of the liberated concentration camps will probably never be fully appreciated.

The number of homes that were salvaged by padres are innumerable. Hundreds of tormented men received malicious letters from well-meaning friends and were on the point of breaking up their marriage. The padres saved the day.

I know that these eminent churchmen will forgive me if I skip their present titles and refer to them as we knew them as our padres. I bring to mind such staunch workers as Padres Ross Flemington,

Maurice Roy, Mike O'Neill, Norman McCall, and hundreds of others.

The troops of the First War, of course, had great padres too. Many of them have now passed on to their just reward. I suppose the most outstanding name in that gallant company would be that of the beloved Canon Scott of the Old Red Patch, who gave so much of himself to humanity.

The evening was well advanced towards midnight when the padre and myself reluctantly broke up the memory feast. "Do you ever play cribbage now, padre?" I asked. "Cribbage, cribbage," he mused as if savouring a delectable morsel. "No, I don't. What I wouldn't give for a rousing four-handed game of cribbage."

As I walked into the night, he closed the door. He also closed the door on the life behind. Once more he was the village clergyman. But he would always be a man — a real man.

The Day we Beat the Yanks

GIVE a Canadian soldier an acre of ground, a softball or a football and you've got yourself a ball game. Within six minutes you've also got yourself a bunch of rooters who make the Brooklyn fans sound like old maids at a game of drop-the-hanky.

Believe me, I know what I'm talking about. I remember attending a softball game around this time years ago. The stalwarts were those fighting footsloggers of D-Day fame, the Queen's Own Rifles, and the 2nd Echelon team from Germany.

More than 7,000 screaming supporters packed the Ajax Stadium in Amsterdam. The way those guys were laying down side bets of guilders, francs, Woodbines, Lugers and good old army blankets put the World Series gamblers in the kindergarten class.

The 2nd Echelon boys were game but no match for the C.F.N. and Armed Forces champs. I don't know if Brigadier Jock Sprague was on hand or not that particular day. But he must have done a war dance on his game leg when he heard the score of 8-0 in favour of his Queen's Own boys. The big gun of the day was the booming bat of short-stop Doug Adam who rapped out three hits for as many runs.

When the high brass blew the final whistle to stop shooting the Jerries, they found themselves with a rootin', tootin' bunch of boisterous mavericks on their hands. Wisely they let the boys see Paree and get the parlour rugby games out of their system. Then they settled down to a solid sports program. The boys ate it up.

Football came into its own. The 4th and 5th Div squads, the Army Troops and others started to punt the pigskin around. I didn't see too many of these games. At that time of the year I was nervously pacing up and down the rattling floorboards of a Nissen hut awaiting shipping news. But I do remember the boys working out at the Water Rats stadium in Utrecht. A real booter with the Army Troops was a husky gent named "Sag" Segalowitz, a former Ottawa Rough Rider and Montreal Bulldog.

The football session, though, that really stands out was held in London around late 1943. By this time the Yanks had arrived in large numbers. The Canadians — good, clean sporting types — had the Piccadilly and Leicester Square area pretty well staked out for their own private entertainment. Then along came Uncle Sam's boys just loaded with spondulicks. Without as much as "by your leave" they told the Canucks to "move over". This was a most unwise declaration. Most unwise.

Naturally this led to numerous "I seen her first" discussions. These were promptly settled on the spot without all of the Marquis of Queensbury rules being observed. Forthright the brain department at C.M.H.Q. got the brilliant idea of letting the boys settle their disputes on the field of honour. And what more mutual ground than a good old North American football field?

There was only one hitch. Both countries called it football but each had different rules. After burning the midnight oil, a compromise was reached. They would play one half Canadian rules and the other under American standards.

Both sides went into secret training. This was big business! A lot of national honour was at stake. Who was to head up the Canadian team? Under normal military procedure it would be at least Brigadier Thingmebub. But even the mightiest realized that this was no time for clinging to the rules of seniority. They went right to the bottom of the ladder and dug up a mere private. They couldn't have made a wiser choice. That private was Gunner Ted Reeves of Connie Smyth's Sporting Battery.

An old rugby great and today the most outstanding sports columnist in Canada, Ted Reeves quickly dug out hidden talent. I wish I could remember all who played on our team. I particularly remember Orville Burke and Andy Tommy, formerly of the Ottawa Rough Riders. I believe that Jeff Nicholson and Fritzie Hanson of the Winnipeg Blue Bombers were also on the team.

Anyhow, the day was bright and clear at White City Stadium. Every Yank and Canuck with red blood was there. Thousands of Union Jacks and Star-Spangled Banners covered the grandstand and surrounding fences. Military bands by the score blared forth, trying to out-Bogey each other. There was more brass in the centre field for the kickoff than Perle Mesta ever dreamed of seeing at one party.

By all the odds of fortune it should have been cradle-snatching for the Yanks. I think we only had three Divisions in England at that time. The other two were either enroute or preparing to go to the Mediterranean. The Americans had hundreds of thousands to pick from. The result is now history. We won the blooming game. We whomped the Yanks at their own specialty.

London was ours that night. I'll never forget the celebration afterwards. Whitehall would never have approved! The brass mingled with the lowly like Kid's Day at the C.N.E. Gunner Ted Reeves was flanked, sought after and hugged by everyone from generals to batmen. Poor Ted. He had been in the army so long he didn't know whether to stand up, salute or rub noses. Finally, in typical fashion, he shrugged it off calling to all, "Hi pals, glad you enjoyed it."

If the Canadians were out celebrating, the Yanks certainly were not. They hadn't been so shocked since the day prohibition was declared. When the news reached the Pentagon, jaws dropped. Drums rolled across the Potomac. Battle plans were forgotten. Coded messages of highest priority flashed across the Atlantic. A return game was requested.

Like the good, clean cut types that we are, imbued with the proper British sporting blood, etc., etc., we accepted. Nothing like giving the vanquished a sporting chance, y'know. That was all the Yanks needed. The might and power of the whole U.S. Armed Forces went into action.

Large transport planes rumbled through the night across the dark Atlantic. Security officers at Gander knew there was something special afoot. But theirs was not to reason why. This cargo was strictly top secret. This particular cargo was dynamite — T.N.T. in the form of Bronc Nagurski and every able-bodied football player the army could dig up in the United States. They tell me they even tried giving Vitamin B shots to Red Grange and Indian Jim Thorpe in case they needed them.

You all know the story of the return match. We lost. But even then we put up a rousing good fight.

Anyhow, apart from the results, these games were good for morale. The Yanks formed a healthy respect for their wee neighbours. They even shared their favourite stamping grounds with us. And that, as you know, was a mighty big concession.

About Nobler Things . . .
Rum; Schnapps; Gin and Vin Rouge

I was lounging in my sack, torturing myself with a paper just received from home. By this time I had wearied of the valiant stories about the hockey teams which had so nobly donated their gate receipts — less expenses — to the cigarette fund. The marriage of the Jobson twins bored me as did the piffle-paffle of patriotic speeches.

What fascinated me most was the double page centre-spread of the grocery store. Pictures of mouth-watering steaks, cantaloupes and tossed salads made me groan. I groaned again when I thought about cook's special for chow that night — large bowel-deadening tinned sausages to be followed three days later by a jet-actioned Number Nine.

Just as I was feeling sorry for myself and cussing the stay-at-homes a red-haired demon named Corporal Edward Stokes barges in. Stokesy was chief hot-rodder of the unit. He always kept a spare rotor in his tunic, just in case he should run into a stray, unattended jeep. "The Old Man wants to see you. Looks like he's powerful worried about something," he says.

I buckled on my web belt, straightened my gaiters, gave a few hard stomps to straighten out the crease and made for the Old Man's quarters. A thousand things flashed through my mind. The Old Man couldn't know about my overstayed leave. Some well-placed favours had fixed that in the orderly room. True, there was a report on the way from the provost about my wearing an American parka and refusing to remove same. But that wasn't too serious.

My old drill instructor at Aldershot would have been proud of me as I gave the Old Man my best guardsman "one-two", ramrod stiff, thumbs back of the seams. The colonel wasn't one bit impressed. He gives me a bored look. The Buckingham Palace presentation was old stuff to a man who had paraded a hundred defaulters.

"At ease, Smith. Have a good Canadian cigarette," he says. I took one and relaxed cautiously. Whenever the Old Man handed out free fags like that you could be prepared for doing something "outside the line of duty".

"Smith," says he, "I don't know what we would do without you. We now have three jeeps, two cycles, one 30 hundredweight and a Volkswagen more than we can draw on our W/E. And, I learn from reliable sources that you—ah—managed to secure them for the unit."

I modestly admitted that I had helped somewhat. Inwardly I was praying that the Old Man wasn't sucking me in to be a fall guy for a DADOS ordnance check-up.

The Colonel cut in on my thoughts. "And, by Gad, sir, it is fortunate that you are good for something, because," and here he paused, fixing me with the gimlet eye, "from other reliable sources I learn that you are doing your damndest to lose this war for us single-handedly."

I panicked, wondering what the Old Man did know. Could it be the blankets that I had flogged on a '48 in Brussels? The copper tubing we had "borrowed" to get a batch of home brew moving?

The Old Man kept the gimlet eye focused on me. Then he turned the tap on and smiled that great big Dale Carnegie special that he usually reserves for the high brass. "Relax, Smithy, relax. I know *puhlenty* about you. But I didn't bring you here to throw the whole of K.R. Can. at you."

He continues, "Somewhere on this broad continent there must be a decent drop of liquor. I'm sick and tired of drinking that bath-tub cognac and so is my poor mottled stomach. Where can I get some good liquor without ransoming my children's future to pay for it?"

I stood still and thought fast. It would never do to tell him about the home brew. And besides, perhaps the colonel's tastes didn't run to raw alky, plus a few ingredients that are made primarily to keep transport vehicles from freezing up.

I shrugged, "I really don't know, sir."

The Old Man twisted the tap off something fierce. Gone was the Dale Carnegie smile and on came the thunder clouds. "Like hell you don't," he roared, pounding the table with his ham fist. "You have managed to scrounge everything movable from Courseulles to Nijmegen and now, by Gad, you are going to get some good liquor for this outfit. And that's an order."

I gulped and stammered, "Yes, sir."

"That's better," says he. "Here's five thousand francs, belge. Now go and see the adjutant and get yourself a six-day pass. Tell him I said so and that you are on a roving commission to do a story for *The Maple Leaf.*"

I about-turned on a dime, stepped off briskly on the left foot when he called after me, "And don't you go near Brussels, stay clear of Paris and bring back some good liquor and plenty of it, or else." He left the dire warning hanging in mid-air. But I knew then that the Old Man knew a lot. Too much for comfort.

It might sound good to you blokes to have six days' leave, a jeep and five thousand francs. But you didn't know my Old Man. We had

80 thirsty men in our unit and five thousand francs wasn't going very far. At the prices the highway robbers in Brussels, Antwerp and Paris were charging I would be lucky to get a prescription filled, let alone get enough for the unit.

This the Old Man well knew. So I was on my own with everywhere and yet nowhere to go. It would be a simple thing to make a deal with a connection, but when the Old Man said good liquor, he meant just that and not rotgut. So the connection was out.

Now then, where to go first? I thought about the old stamping grounds. Up the Scheldt along the Flushing Spit? Across the Leopold Canal to Terneuzen? Molentje northeast of Bruges? No, all they ever had was water, water and more water.

s'Hertogenbosch? The British rear echelons had that place drained. Nijmegen? The Canadians had squeezed that salient like a lemon. The fly bomb sites from the Seine to Pas de Calais? After the Second Division got through with liberating Dieppe it was doubtful if even a grape remained untrod.

No, the only promise of solution lay ahead — up with the troops — in the hope that I could get in on a market where the prices were right. By this time the liberation show of each village had developed into a pattern. Liberation, dancing in the streets, *joie de vive,* champagne, and then the settling down period. Six weeks later the bottle of cognac that was handed to you on liberation, and for which the Jerries had paid their own price, cost a monstrous 800 francs.

Four days went by and I had nothing for my pains. Whenever the troops took a town they got first priority on what was available. And that in Holland wasn't much. I finally struck gold in Germany near the Reichswald Forest in a little place called Moyland. It was in the vicinity of the Goch-Calcar-Udem territory.

It is surprising the magic that a few cigarettes can work. A wheedling character when he twigged what I was after told me about a warehouse his uncle was caretaking in the woods. It contained liquor — lots of it, he swore, as he rolled his eyes. He wanted to show me the way. Greeneyed as I was, I wasn't going into the woods alone with this character. I made a deal with two well-equipped infantrymen to tag along — just for the ride.

The guy, though, was on the level. The warehouse was there. And so was the liquor. Lashin's of it, me hearties! Thousands upon thousands of gallons of the stuff. Rum, schnapps, gin, red wine, white wine, all stored in huge glass demi-johns covered in straw casings. And, it was all ours for the asking! All ours, that is, unless one was stupid enough to report it to the proper authorities!!

There was plenty for all. In no time we let an Army Service outfit in on the deal in exchange for the loan of two 60 hundredweights.

No conquering gladiator ever got a more tumultuous welcome home than yours truly. I was the hero of the unit. Five hundred bleedin' gallons worth of hero worship!

The Old Man was in his seventh heaven. If it hadn't been for the presence of the troops I am sure he would have done a jig. He kept calling me, "My boy, my boy." He pounded me on the back and poured himself a shot of rum. Then he froze right there in his tracks. I thought he was going to pass out. Finally he got his breath back and his "my boy" turned to, "My God, I've been poisoned!"

I have imbibed pre-war Newfie screech; smothered on Calvados; smiled in Mexico over their firewater Tequila; skolled Norwegian gin straight; gasped over Brooklyn bourbon, but never have I strangled over anything like that German rum.

The damn stuff was 76 percent overproof! It was the kickapoo joy juice that the German commanders were feeding their troops to drive them over the top.

The Old Man might have thought it was horrible. The troops said it was wonderful. We mollified the Old Man by trading in a few demi-johns for Fancy Dan French liquors which pleased him no end, plus the return of his five thousand francs!

Gazooks, them was the days, fellas! No frantic waving of four fingers at the waiter. Just fill 'er up. A big thirst, a big appetite and big men to help you with them.

"Frenchy"– another Army Character

IT has always been my fortune to fall in with "characters". Then, of course, as the Little Woman always says, "Birds of a feather flock together". Anyhow, I like characters. They make life interesting.

Every "character" who didn't fit in with the "solid" citizens of other units seemed to drift into our outfit. The funny part about it was that, being birds of a feather, they understood each other. In any other company they would be labelled as screwballs. In our gang nobody paid any attention to them. So they went along and did their jobs the way they saw fit and the end result was usually good.

The only one who lost weight and hair was the adjutant. A decent, sensible type, he had to clean up the paper mess afterwards. "Adj" was always bemoaning his fate and praying for a transfer.

One day he tried to be a good guy and go along with the boys for a ride. They took him in a Bren carrier to see the Big Show up ahead. They got lost. Worse, they got captured. Luckily the Boche turned out to be conscripted Balkanites with no special love for Der Fuhrer. They took one look at our compo rations, said, *"Schnitzlle on the Fritzlle"*, and kameraded to get in on the Allied feed-bag. After that "Adj" stuck to his paper work.

I had almost forgotten some of the characters when out of the blue came a Christmas card from "Frenchy" MacDonald. "Frenchy" was as Frenchy as they make them. He hailed from Outremont. In spite of his Scotch surname he didn't know a haggis from a plum pudding.

Frenchy rode through the last show like a tourist with a million bucks couldn't imitate. He was style all the while. And he treated the war as a Coney Island holiday. Don't get him wrong. He was no slacker. He landed at Courseulles on D-Day. And he picked up a wound stripe plus a M.I.D. But to him life was a bowl of cherries just waiting for him to gorge on.

Frenchy and myself were standing outside the Abbey aux Hommes in Caen. The troops had broken through across the Orne. The Trun-Chambois sector was a shambles. Where the front line was nobody knew. Headquarters moved several times in one day. Bewildered commanders were saying, "Where's Brigade?" Brigade was saying, "Where's Div?" Div. didn't even know where Corps was.

Says Frenchy, "Hey, Smeety, what t'hell we 'ang aroun' for. Let us go." So away we went after the pack. We finally came to a halt in Lisieux.

Lisieux as I remember it was a pretty town with green, sloping hills all around. On the top of a hill was a beautiful structure — a shrine called St. Theresa's. It reminded me a lot of Brother Andre's shrine in Montreal.

However, just as we were admiring the view, the Jerries zeroed in with their 88's. We decided to scram and leave what was left of the town to the British 51st Division who were mopping up patches in the nearby woods.

On the way back the motor conked out. Frenchy volunteered to mosey down the lane to a farming village to clean out the carburettor. An hour passed and no sign of Frenchy. Throwing my last Woodbine in the ditch I cursed him and jogged down the dusty lane.

Was Frenchy cleaning out the carburettor? No sir. He was cleaning out the last of a bottle of vin rouge! He was happy as a pig in clover. The French villagers off the beaten path had been by-passed by the troops. They wanted to celebrate their liberation, only they didn't have a guest of honour. And what better guest could they have than a compatriot who not only spoke French but whose grandmother (he said) had come from Normandy?

My French was strictly of the vooley-voo type. But it didn't matter. All they wanted was someone to wine and dine. We figured it was our patriotic duty to fill in for the unavoidable absence of His Majesty, Winston Churchill, General Montgomery and anybody else they cared to toast.

Hours later, stuffed with rare steaks, huge buttered beans washed down with cider, cognac, calvados and champagne, we left the cheering villagers enroute for Caen. A good Norman mechanic had fixed the carburettor and put it on.

We didn't make Caen that night. We ended up by bivouacking in an orchard. A mobile ack-ack battery set up shop in the next field. The boys banged away for several hours that night. We didn't hear a thing.

A few days later we ended up in Rouen. The British had taken over. In the meanwhile the Essex Scottish, the R.H.L.I.'s and the Royal Regiment of Canada were hightailing towards Dieppe, prepared to pay off an old debt.

We Cooks-toured the lovely city of Rouen. We said a prayer in the magnificent Rouen cathedral. Later, in a cafe, we bought some "feelthy pictures". Such is the Jekyll and Hyde in us all.

Rouen was in a stage where one mode of law and order had ceased and no new one was established. However, a strict curfew was established at night for obvious reasons.

At two ack emma we left our hosts and felt our way along in the blacked-out streets. We were lost. And not a soul was in sight. We knocked on doors but we knocked in vain. After four years of listening to Gestapo bangings after midnight, the good people of Rouen weren't answering any doorbells.

I lost Frenchy somewhere along the darkened streets and was prepared to curl up in a doorway for the night. Suddenly my hair stood on end and I nearly jumped out of my tunic when the silence was shattered by a rapid burst of gunfire.

Doors flew open. Windows flew up. F.F.I.'s scrambled out, tucking in their shirts, guns at the alert and trigger-itchy. I followed the sound of the guns. There, in the middle of a huge square, was Frenchy. High over his head was his Sten gun rat-tat-tatting to the heavens.

By this time a crowd had milled around. They wanted to know where the sal Boche were. Frenchy was all smiles. There were no Boche, he explained. He merely wanted to know where his quarters were on la rue Rheims.

An excited crowd escorted him back jabbering away in French. I tagged along shaking my head at his method of direction-finding.

It seems that Frenchy did O.K. for himself after the war. His Christmas card was postmarked from Brussels. He had returned and married Mademoiselle Yvette Therien. Yvette's papa owns a big cafe near the place Bruchere. But papa has retired to Deauville, and guess who runs the show?

Frenchy's message was typical, "Come on over, sucker, and quit working. I give you a good job. You can handle my upstairs department."

Blessings on you, Frenchy.

Sidekicks

I wonder what has happened to Slim Taylor? A guy with a big heart, big fists — and a big temper.

I suppose each of you blokes came out of the services with fond memories of some sidekick you liked especially well, the kind of guy you enjoyed spending a 48 in London with. . . One of you had nine pounds ten, the other twelve quid even. The difference never mattered. When one was broke, the other forked over half of what he had left. Such a guy was Slim.

How many Slims, Spuds, Bucks, Nobbys, Smittys, Frenchys and just plain Joes are there scattered across the country? Fellows you knew and liked and have never heard of since. I often wonder if we would have the same in common today that we had in those stimulating days. Perhaps it is just as well that we remember each other in the fond way we do.

I'd like to tell you more about Slim. I am convinced that today he is either on top or in jail. He was that sort of guy. No half measures.

I first ran into Slim at Leatherhead. Any of you blokes been to Leatherhead? One day it was a quiet "off the map" village. The next day H.Q. 1st Canadian Army set up shop there. Overnight the quiet little village was swamped as trucks rolled down the winding streets, engulfed the garages and spilled a flow of khaki out on to the pavements.

Slim was the noisiest of the lot, but the first to be taken into a local home. I think he completely fascinated the sedate and nice English couple. However, it took quite some time for the good lady to find out why Slim shied away from her home-cooking: Secretly he loved it, but he didn't figure it right to be eating their rations.

About four pence ha'penny away from Leatherhead was the even smaller village of Stoneleigh. It never ceased to amaze me how far you could travel on these English trains for a couple of those penny cart-wheels.

Stoneleigh on a Saturday night was something to remember. A retired boxer named Arthur Smith ran a combined pub, billiard room and dance hall. Arthur today should be driving a gold-plated Rolls Royce. The troops just flocked there, and the lassies from nearby Epsom did likewise.

To get a drink at the bar was quite a feat. Arms kept thrusting one pound notes which the barmaids completely ignored. Finally one of them would say, "What'll it be, ducky? Whisky? You gone balmy, love? Ere, 'ave a Worthington."

But not Slim. If Slim wanted whisky, it was whisky he got. Somewhere, somehow the barmaids found it when Slim called. A dozen arms outstretched pleading for refills would all be ignored if Spud just raised his hand. I could never figure it out but was sure glad to bask in his company.

It wasn't until months later, bivouacked near Carpiquet, that I managed to wangle from Slim the secret of his success with the barmaids.

"Elementary, my dear Smith," says he. "You want something and it's hard to get. So you stop shoving and use your bean instead."

"What," he says, "in wartime England is the mostest thing a married barmaid would like to have?"

"I dunno," says I. "Her husband?"

"Stupid," says he. "They got kids and kids like eggs. Only they can't get eggs."

"That figgers," says I.

"Now then," he continues. "What is it a farmer likes most that he can't get?"

"Fertilizer?" says I.

"Bright boy," Slim growls. "Nah, cigarettes, ya chump. I give the farmer some fags, he gives me some eggs, and I slip the hen-fruit to the barmaid for free. Guess who's the white-haired boy after that?"

As I said before, Slim today is either right on top or else in jail.

Slim was brave to the point of being foolhardy. Several times I watched him wander into apple orchards near Falaise that bore signs marked "These verges have not been cleared". And all to get a helmet full of sour, green apples.

Weeks later I was to see a new and different side to Slim. We both ended up in a hospital that was just outside of Bayeaux. Gad, how the years play havoc with the memory! But I believe this particular hospital was No. 7 General.

As I said before, Slim was a pretty brave guy. But there was one gal who really had his number. She was a nursing sister we used to call Sister Red. Her flaming red hair, freckled face and large, grinning mouth was a tonic to watch in action. Every morning she came to Slim's bed with a large hypodermic needle in her hands, "O.K., boy," she'd say. "Roll over."

Slim would take one look at that long needle and the colour would drain from his face. A Jerry or two he could face. But that needle . . . oi, oi, oi! It almost became a wrestling match each morning for Sister Red to get him to bare his buttock. Eventually Slim would give in, roll over, grit his teeth, close his eyes and wait for the stab. Meantime the rest of us would be sitting up in bed making smart remarks and go into gales of laughter when Sister Red plunged the needle home.

Came the time when Slim was recuperating and feeling chipper again. True to his policy of "let's get organized" he made fast friends with a hospital orderly. Within a few days he was having little extras smuggled in.

Came also the time when Sister Red comes around to take temperatures. Slim's temperature is not only high but he himself is higher than a kite, thanks to a smuggled-in bottle of Calvados.

"All right, wise guy," says she. "Hand over the bottle."

"What bottle?" says Slim innocently.

"Oh, cut the guff, soldier," says Red, "and hand it over."

Meantime Slim is thinking fast but the Calvados has slowed him down so he isn't thinking too good.

"Try and get it," shouts Slim triumphantly as he shoves the bottle down between his legs. As I said before, Slim is not thinking very good. Naively he figures, with male modesty, that Sister Red would never dare trespass on the spot where he has the bottle hidden.

Sister Red is no longer fooling. With one hefty arm she thrusts beneath the sheets and grabs.

"Ouch!" screams Slim, his face going red as blood.

Sister Red blushes too. It seems her first thrust has not been entirely accurate!

Undaunted she returns to the fray. And this time she brings forth the bottle of Calvados. The fight is gone out of Slim. He is too flabbergasted for words.

I wonder where Slim Taylor is today? I wonder also where Sister Red is? Neither of them won the war single-handed. But to me they were nice people. People I would like to see again.

Memories of "the Major"

IF someone was to ask you the question, "Do nice guys or nasty guys get along best in the services?" what would be your answer?

If you were to say, "In my opinion nice guys go further," then that settles the argument . . . or does it?

I well remember a few years back when Field-Marshal Montgomery, attending the funeral of an old classmate from Sandhurst, was asked this question by reporters, "How was it that the deceased started off on an equal footing and had better marks than you at Sandhurst but only wound up as a lieutenant-colonel and you rose to the very top?"

Monty, in his typical forthright manner, came back without any hesitation, "That is not too difficult to answer, Colonel Sampson was too nice a chap to go very far in the army."

And that, my friends, was a statement from one who really knew what it takes to get ahead in the services.

This brings me along to memories of The Major. There were a half a dozen majors in our outfit. They all had names such as Major Phelps, Major Crowthers, Major Ramsey. But always the boys referred to Major Graham as simply "The Major", and everybody knew whom we were talking about. He was that kind of a guy.

Looking back now, perhaps it was his maturity plus his M.M. and bar from the First World War that caused a certain amount of hero worship in our ranks.

Usually if an officer had the gall to walk into a sergeant's mess without being invited he got a pretty cool reception. Not so The Major. At any time of the day he could poke his head in and say, "Do you mind if I come in," and instantly blokes sprang to their feet to offer him a chair.

The Major was the kind who, when sitting in a seven hand game of draw, would look at your diminishing pile of chips and say, "Could you use a few hundred francs until your luck turns?"

I first ran into The Major when we were in the marshalling area south of Southampton waiting our turn to be fed to the ships through the "sausage machine".

There was a hitch in our progress. It seems we were there way ahead of schedule. So, army-like, they clamped us into a security area in a wooded estate surrounded by barbed wire.

Meantime a driver named Cornell went over the hill. Three days later he returned under his own steam. The adjutant was all for hauling out the book . . . section this, section that; desertion in time of war, etcetera. If they had lashed Cornell to a gun wheel I would not have been surprised.

And then The Major stepped in. In a quiet voice he called Cornell to his tent for a man-to-man chat. Sometime later he spoke to the adjutant. "I will take full responsibility for Cornell's future conduct. As O.C. of this unit I will set the punishment instead of referring it to the C.O."

Cornell, it turned out, had left his sweetheart in Leatherhead, unwed and expecting a baby. He had scampered back to marry his woman and then scampered back to Southampton again.

The Major, according to the book, was way off base in his military handling of the situation. But then, as I said before, he was that kind of a guy.

A few weeks later we set up headquarters at an elaborate spot in Courseulles that had been used by the German staff. The chateau, complete with concrete and steel roof and the orchard honeycombed with air-raid shelters, made us feel pretty snug and secure.

However, the Jerries had this all figured out. They knew the layout like a soldier knows his pay book and proceeded to stonk the area with great gusto. It was then that a well-known war correspondent suffering what we all felt, a desperate sort of fear, lost control completely and ran screaming down the road.

For two days he was a babbling mess. During those two days it was The Major who kept him under sedatives and refused to ship him back to the U.K. To send him back would have meant disgrace. The Warco finally got hold of himself and went on for the rest of the war doing a bang-up job.

But June and July of '44, although noted for its front line casualties, brought forth another enemy — dysentery. With water supplies polluted by dead and bloated animals, and bulging blue-bottle flies swarming on your food in clusters, No. 7 Canadian General Hospital near Bayeaux was soon crowded to the tent flaps.

The Major, fifty years of age and greying fast, had lost twenty pounds in three weeks. Weak and peaked he used to joke that he was like a good poker hand — "open at both ends".

He refused to go to the hospital, fearing that at his age they would ship him home. Meantime he ran his unit from a stretcher.

All through the Falaise Gap debacle and the rat-race across France and Belgium The Major held on and triumphed over his age.

It was around s'Hertogenbosch that we settled down for a breather. It was also at s'Hertogenbosch that The Major's luck ran out.

The Germans, rallying, were trying to establish a line across south-west Holland running from Bergen through Roosendaal to Breda, Tilburg and s'Hertogenbosch.

This was polder country trooped by panzer grenadiers. Now the rumour had it they were being reinforced by paratroops from across the Rhine estuary and scheduled to attack s'Hertogenbosch.

The usual alarms were on. The Major, trying as usual to set an example by leading, had not slept for two days. With the alarm at its highest, who should pop in for a quick look but the C.O. of the group. And where was The Major? The poor guy had fallen asleep but before doing so had taken a few nips. It was the bottle that the C.O. spotted first. And it was the wrong conclusion that he drew.

Right or wrong, Army is army. And so he woke The Major and gave him round merry hell; this would be his last warning, etcetera.

This must have been around November of '44. The next place we set up camp was at Nijmegen.

You blokes will remember the long, frosty and dismal wait we had in Nijmegen. There was a complete stalemate and it looked as if we were never going to move along.

All of us by this time (which was near mid-January of '45) had taken a 72 in Brussels or Paris. But not The Major. Not a day off had he taken.

It was then he decided to take a quick run down to Paris, see the sights and buy a bottle of perfume for the missus.

Let's face it. An old soldier like The Major should have known better than to scamper off without first checking with his C.O. who was camped some miles away. But then he probably figured as O.C. of his unit he had certain rights.

There's no doubt about it that Lady Luck really turned her capricious head away from The Major. That very day, who should arrive at our unit but the C.O. and four of Canada's leading publishers on a two weeks' Cook's Tour of the front lines.

To make matters worse the sentry, a new reinforcement, was caught playing cards with the cook, and the officer of the day was nowhere to be found.

To add further fuel to the fire one of the publishers, a would-be war correspondent, wrote a first person story about the Canadian unit that was virtually unguarded and the O.C. on a spree in Paris.

This was the end. The C.O. was mortified and the army was embarrassed. And so in cold fury they shipped The Major home.

Never have I seen a man look so forlorn. The end of the road for an old soldier who received absolutely no marks at all for the tough sledding behind him.

Do good guys get ahead? Do nasty guys succeed? I don't know. The army seems so far away these days I no longer feel an authority on the matter.

But this much I do know. I feel good. Real good, deep down inside. I have just finished reading an item from a small town newspaper which tells about The Major being selected as Mr. Good Citizen of the Year.

And of this I am certain. In selecting The Major, the citizens knew not nor cared naught about what it read in King's Rules and Regulations of the years 1939 to 1945.

The Biggest Bash in History

ABOUT this time of the year we can cogitate on the anniversary of the biggest bash in history. Around midnight on May 8, 1945, there were enough hangovers in the making to keep the seltzer and aspirin tycoons in luxury for the rest of their bicarbonated lives.

Not so long ago a bunch of us were at the Legion hall, quietly — as befitting our years — quaffing a few draughts of beer. I looked around the group and pondered how the years had mellowed the "terrors of yesteryear".

Take Joe, balding, pleasantly overweight and contented as a Piccadilly Commando the day after pay day. Fifteen years ago when Joe entered a pub, the owner automatically reached for his wooden mallet. It wasn't that Joe was vicious. He just plain loved to raise merry hell.

Then he met Mary of Guildford, a pint-sized dream who, Joe felt, needed protection. Fourteen years and three kids later I began to wonder who needed to protect who. Because somewhere, somehow, along the line little Mary had converted Joe the heller into Joe the domestic to beat all domestics.

Anyhow, the chit-chat swung around towards the big bash of May 8. Like old braves around the campfire each buckaroo in turn chortled over his contribution to that hectic day.

Joe was on leave in the U.K. the day when word flashed around the world that the war in Europe was over. I guess all of the Western group went a little wacky that day. The U.K. was no exception. But let Joe tell his version:

"I was doing my drinking down around the Haymarket. The place was going mad. You couldn't get a drink if your old man owned the joint, so I lit out to see the sights.

"London was one big bonfire. There must have been hundreds of them. It was the first time I had seen London so bright since the big fire-raising raids of 1940. When they couldn't get enough wood to keep the fires roaring, they tore down the billboards of the theatres.

"Up around Piccadilly Circus thousands danced in the street, formed circles, waved flags and sang, "There'll Always Be An England". I'll never forget a bus trying to edge through the crowd, with three Aussies and four R.A.F. types doing a war dance on the roof.

"The pubs went dry, so everybody took to the streets. Trafalgar Square was jammed so tight even the pigeons couldn't land. There was one bloke with a banjo sitting at the foot of one of Nelson's lions while a group of girls danced around him.

"VE-Day was just about the soberest one I ever spent," said Joe. "Mind you, I was plastered by three o'clock and sobered by six o'clock for the simple reason nobody, but nobody, had any liquor left to sell. Anyhow, it's a ruckus I won't ever forget in a hurry," he concluded with a gentlemanly sip of his beer.

Just waiting to get his two cents in was Nobby Clarke. Nobby had been on convoy escort out of Halifax and was in that troop-shattered city when the news flashed in.

"I dunno, I can't account for it," said Nobby. "A real hysteria seemed to take hold that nobody could control. At first it just seemed good, clean fun to go out, buy a crock and raise hell. But if anybody was to tell me that this shindig was going to wind up with $5,000,000 damage I wouldn't have believed him.

"I was in the liquor store on Hollis street and the mob was a thousand deep. Everybody had the same idea: get a bottle, get five if possible; then go out and get drunk. The poor jokers behind the counter were going nuts. The crowd got impatient, broke up the queues and the pushing soon became chaotic.

"The pressure was on and something had to give. I think the lid blew off when a clerk banged his cash drawer shut and said, 'That's all for now. We're not serving any more until the store is cleared.'

"With that, a big red-headed sailor said, 'On a pig's eye you're closing! I came here to get likker, and likker I'm going to get.' With that, others took up the roar. The big sailor jumped over the counter and fifty men followed him. Within twenty minutes they had gutted that store out. The first shot had been fired.

"The police were powerless to interfere. Each time the patrol wagons came on the scene, the boys turned them over and set them on fire. Finally the cops gave up and went home.

"I think up to that point we could call it good, clean fun," said Nobby, "but all that liquor was too much for the boys to handle. If they had left it at that point it might have died a natural. But then some guys got the idea of raiding the brewery. This they did, 500 of them.

"Within one hour thousands of cases of beer were dumped on the pavements and the boys drank beer by the dozen bottles. It was a drunk the like of which I will never see again, or want to. Even that wouldn't have been so bad if they had left the stores alone. But not content with booze, they went wild and began smashing store windows, looting goods, burning doors and generally raising hell."

We solemnly agreed that the Halifax incident did not do the Canadian serviceman any credit at all.

As for my own contribution towards VE-Day I can, modestly, record only a minor part that will not excite the historians.

We had put *The Maple Leaf* to bed in Brussels, the front page reading simply KAPUT! The news wires between our plant and Rheims were burning frenziedly for 48 hours and we quietly opened a demi-john. "A demi-john?" queried one of the boys. "What t'heck is that?" "That, my fine feathered friend," says I, "is a large glass jar completely covered with protective straw netting and holding approximately 10 gallons of German naval rum." I then proceeded to enlighten the boys as follows:

"While the boys in the U.K. were going tongue-dry for a drink, we had no less than 20 demi-johns of this Nazi kickapoo juice. Real goof syrup it was, too. Pure, unadulterated raw alcohol that they fed the U-boat mariners to keep their courage up.

"I came across the stuff near Wilhelmshaven in a big warehouse when I was looking for newsprint. Naturally I felt that it needed some solid Canadian protection."

"Naturally," the boys solemnly agreed.

"Walking in Brussels that night was only possible at a snail's pace. I finally made the Metropole Hotel. The lounge was filled with soldiers and pretty A.T.S. girls lifting bottles of beer and shouting out the choruses of 'Bless 'Em All', 'Roll Me Over In The Clover', 'If I Had My Way', etc. The surprising part was that, drunk or sober, they sang the clean versions!

"And then what happened?" the group chorused.

"And then, my friends, sad to relate, I was possessed of a warm, comfy and drowsy feeling as Hitler's joy-juice took command.

"In a far corner there was a nice stuffed chair. I sank deep into the depth of its broken springs, waved a feeble hand aloft and, with a fuzzy 'Huzzah for the bloody British!' I passed pleasantly out."

The boys all nodded in sympathetic understanding.

"Swifty"

THERE is only one thing wrong with pay-days: the ruddy things are too far apart. It was ever thus in the service. For two days a month you were flush, the other twenty-eight stony broke.

I notice a slight difference in civvy street. Instead of being flush two days a month I am broke thirty days. Whereas in 1940 there were single pairs of hands waiting for the few quid I owed them, nowadays it seems that many octopuses stretch forth and snatch my miserable pittance before I can call it my own.

I was mulling the problem over recently on the idea of making a quick buck, which is something that has always fascinated me. It fascinated me in the services. It also fascinated the other boys in the unit. Whenever they wanted to make a few quick bucks they always invited me to their poker sessions.

I used to pride myself on my poker face. I had only one drawback. Whenever I drew anything higher than a pair of tens, my hands would shake, my face go red and my eyes light up like neon signs. I had more friends on pay nights than any six guys in the Nissen hut. The rest of the thirteen days between pay parades the wise guys used to seize my wrist watch as collateral before they would deal me a hand.

It's a funny thing but some guys were just born to win. And others who convinced themselves they were hot-shots were just as bound to lose. I imagine that if you blokes look back on the fellas in your units you can pinpoint some characters who always seemed to come out on top with a fistful of dough.

Such a character was Swifty. I first ran into Swifty when we were idling away the days at Debert waiting for a boat to go across the big pond. In a hut at Debert the boys with the bank roll and a deck of cards always seemed to be the centre of attraction. Usually they would rack up some sort of table, spread a blanket and they were in business. They seemed to provide a terrific fascination for the small fry who cluttered around watching the big spenders go into operation.

One thing impressed me visibly: we all drew down the same pay. I was always broke, yet somehow a few choice jokers could always produce a sizeable roll to keep them in the game and freeze us poor penny-anters out in the cold.

Swifty was one of the boys with a hefty wad of bills. In keeping with that wad of bills was a big cigar that he chewed on in big-time fashion. I wonder why it is that large cigars and big operators seem to go together. Whenever I smoke on the the blame things I feel kingsize for the first few puffs, and after that just plain anxious to see the end of it.

For some unknown reason Swifty took a hankering to me. It could not be the measly few quid that he won from me. Whenever we went on leave it was Swifty who paid the shot many times over when I was flat broke.

All I know is my stock went up many notches in the unit whenever I said, "Me and Swifty went on leave" . . . "Boy, what a double date me and Swifty had" . . . "Me and Swifty did this" . . . "Me and Swifty did that". Swifty was a big shot in our unit. You travelled in his company, and some of it rubbed off on you.

You blokes remember the panic in those days to get you on your way? Finish a course, a short leave home, then rush, rush, rush like mad to get you on the train. You arrive at a place like Debert all out of breath. Ten days later you are still there and nobody seems to know when you will move, if ever. Ask the orderly room and they look mysterious as if they and only they knew, but they couldn't possibly entrust such vital information to you poor sods.

Now and then, to get you out of their hair, they eked out 48-hour passes. Not long enough to go home but long enough to get into trouble. Only you didn't get into much trouble. By this time you were flat broke.

After three such 48's it shaped up that as drafts kept moving out, ours couldn't be too far behind. It was on such a 48 that Swifty and me wandered down Barrington Street in Halifax.

"Smitty," says he, "I would like to do a little shopping in Eaton's. Come along in."

I figured he was loco. What could a guy possibly want to buy in a department store? Especially when all the money he had was barely enough to cover six quarts of beer and the tram fare to take a gal home after the hostel dance.

I was even more dumbfounded when Swifty wandered into the toy department. I sashayed off to look at some bright new neckties, wondering when I would ever get a chance to wear one again. Five minutes later Swifty walked out whistling, with a small box under his arm.

All he would tell me was that he had made a small purchase and it had cost him close on one dollar.

"You did?" I practically screamed at him. "You mean to tell me that you blew nearly a whole buck of our bundle on a lousy toy?"

Swifty gives me a pitying look. "Son," says he, "this here little toy is gonna make me a rich man. You just wait and see."

Six days later we were easing out of Bedford Basin and away into the broad Atlantic.

It was then that Swifty came into his own. He sidled into the big lounge, casually unwrapped his toy and laid it out on the table. The toy turned out to be a two-foot square of canvas, with little printed symbols like hearts, clubs, crowns, anchors, etc. The name read Crown Anchor. It should have read, "Hiya, Suckers!"

You fellas remember the monotony and boredom of those trips. The main qualification for a transport officer seemed to be a background in the sardine industry. How several thousand souls were expected to cram into facilities normally planned for several hundred beats all reckoning. But they did it.

So there you have a herd squeezed together with nothing to do. A guy like Swifty produces a little diversion. Next thing you know they are pushing like mad to lay down their dimes, quarters and halves on favourite spades, crowns or hearts.

Swifty starts the game off slow and then gradually warms it up. The fever being instilled, he eliminates the penny-anters and only accepts bets of half a buck up to five bucks. In no time at all the small fry are broke. By the time the grey granite houses of Greenock hove into view, Swifty was two thousand dollars to the good on that original one dollar investment!

A week later we went our separate ways on leave, Swifty to London, me to Aberdeen to visit a close relative.

Ten days later the unit got together and Swifty appeared one day late. Again, I was flat broke. So what more natural thing than to hit up my well-heeled friend for a few quid.

I made the pitch. Swifty looked embarrassed and shook his head. "No can do, Smitty. Sorry, but I'm out of dough."

"You're what?" I yelled.

"I'm broke . . . got no mazuma," says he.

"Oh, come now," says I, "you're kidding. You can't tell me that you blew two thousand bucks in ten days. It just can't be done."

"Oh, can't it?" says Swifty. And then he unfolded the sad tale. My leave had been serene. His had been hectic. Swifty had contracted dog fever. Not the love of man's best friend but a whole ten days enjoying the blessed freemasonry of the tracks. In ten days he was already "one of the boys" at Clapton, White City and Harringay.

"I'm telling you," says Swifty with a mad light in his eyes, "this dog racing is the greatest ever. I know I been took. But now I'm getting on the inside. Soon I'll know which dog is going to win in advance. I'll know which dogs are doped and which dogs are hot. I'll . . ." and he rambled on excitedly about his new-found stroke of luck.

No mention, no regrets of the two thousand bucks gone to the dogs. Only hope and anticipation lay ahead.

I haven't seen Swifty since '44. I wonder how he is doing in civvy street? How are all the Big Spenders doing that we once knew? I don't see many of them around any more.

Gals at War

SOMETIME I would love to be a little bird and listen in to a gang of women vets recalling their service days. I'll wager the girls have an anecdote or two that would stand up in any barrack-room exchanges!

During my sojourn on His Majesty's payroll I ran into many sweet young things in khaki or blue. I guess the ladies, bless 'em, always put on their bestest front for the boys just like we did for them.

The one and only time that I saw how the ladies in uniform could really operate was at Uxbridge.

Uxbridge, you air force types will remember, was a R.A.F. depot in Middlesex, not too far from London. The buildings there even put Aldershot to shame for ancient vintage and bore names like Baghdad, Bloemfontein, and other of military-historical background.

One look at the straight iron slats instead of springs in the beds, plus the three concrete-hard biscuit mattresses and you knew that Kipling wasn't fooling when he talked about the lot of Tommy Atkins.

However, the most pleasant aspect of Uxbridge was the presence of literally hundreds upon hundreds of charming young W.A.A.F.'s.

This co-habitation in the same barrack area was far too heady a wine for 500 young Canadian bloods reared on training grounds with a ratio of 98 males to two females.

Naturally they went seeking outlets to demonstrate their manly charms. And the place made to order for such an occasion was the local jive and Lambeth Walk hall, located, I believe, on the main street of Uxbridge under the name of Burton's.

To our sanctimonious surprise Burton's was hopping and rearing to go with a tea dance on a Sunday afternoon.

The idea that dear, dear staid old England would be having a dance on a Sunday afternoon just about shocked our pureblood souls. Alas, we had much to learn and unlearn about our preconceived notions of the English way of life.

It was there that I first met Marj. Full name: Corporal Marjorie Hayward of Nottingham. A card was Marj. A real card. The kind you could crack a joke with and still feel she hadn't lost her bearing in the telling.

It was Marj. who introduced Sgt. Terry Learning, R.C.A.F., of Toronto to AW Penelope Harding, of the Isle of Wight.

This doesn't sound very exciting, but it is necessary that we know the principals before we get along with the story.

I suppose it was inevitable that young impressionable Terry Learning, aged nineteen and one half, should fall in love with young, receptive Penelope, barely nineteen years old.

It was also not too strange that at times, searching for that solitude, that precious privacy that young lovers crave, they should search out the rabbit warrens.

You old codgers remember the rabbit warrens? These, bless you, were the small air raid shelters scattered about the station for quick cover if a surprise air raid took place.

Of varying sizes, they were little more than deep trenches in the ground, with hard benches along the sides to sit on.

Now then, we'll skip this scene and come to the villain of the piece.

The villain in this case was no less a personage than a sergeant-major of the W.A.A.F.'s.

I have met many sergeant-majors in the services, many of them fine people. But there were others, and you all knew them, who felt the moment they got the crown or leaves on their sleeve it gave them a special licence to act and behave like proper s.o.b.'s.

W.O.1 Alice Crindle (that's not her real name, of course) was the female counterpart of this particular breed.

Whether she just plain hated men or all people in general we will never know.

Anyhow, on this particular night, returning to barracks she saw in the dim shadow of the blackout an airman and airwoman disappearing into a rabbit warren.

Quietly she tippy-toed forward. Patiently she waited a few minutes. Then, at the opportune time, she swooped down into the rabbit warren, clicked on her pin point flashlight and caught the young lovers Terry and Penelope in a compromising position.

Need I describe the horror, the utter consternation of the young couple writhing under the whip-lash tongue of the acidulous martinet?

Suffice it is to say that within 24 hours the young airwoman stood red-facedly before her Officer Commanding and in shocked tears heard she was being shipped home to her parents in disgrace, subject to the ultimate decision of the authorities.

The news of Penelope's so-called disgrace ran through the ranks quicker than the clerks could cut the stencils for Daily Routine Orders.

Feelings ran high and men muttered dire threats against the over-officious warrant officer.

But sometimes men mutter in their beards and oftimes we underestimate the primeval power of revenge in the opposite sex.

Within hours a plot was hatching. Hands off, was the signal given to the men. This was a women's problem and it would be resolved by women.

Plot leader was our old friend Corporal Marj Hayward.

A few nights later, as a bomber's moon shone through the clouds, several shadowy figures hovered near the path leading to the women's quarters.

Approaching the quarters was W.O.1 Alice Crindle blithely unaware that danger lurked nearby.

On a given signal three stalwart W.A.A.F.'s pounced upon the unsuspecting warrant officer. Within seconds her muffled cries were lost as struggling they bore her down the nearest rabbit warren.

In grim silence, as if on a pre-rehearsed program, the W.O.1 was bent over a bench. In moments a wooden ladle stolen from the kitchen was whomping her exalted posterior.

Each W.A.A.F. in turn applied the ladle with satisfying vengeance and sturdy enthusiasm.

Then, as quickly and silently as they had come, they disappeared into the night.

To say that there was hell to pay on the station the next day would be putting it mildly.

The O.C., determined to bring the culprits to task and secretly suspecting the reason for the lambasting, questioned all and sundry.

There was one small hitch. The W.O.1 could not identify anyone . . . all had worn gas masks.

But hold! She had noticed a set of corporal's stripes on one arm and the build of the girl looked suspiciously to her like that of Corporal Marjorie Hayward.

In due course a runner presented Corporal Marj before the grim-faced O.C., with the more grim-faced W.O.1 standing by.

"Hayward," says the O.C. "You probably know why you are here. Just where were you around the time that Warrant Officer Crindle was assaulted?"

"Well, ma'am," says Marj demurely, "I really don't know at what time of the night this so-called attack took place."

"For your information, Hayward," says the O.C., "it was just a few minutes before curfew time at 2230 hours."

"Hmmm," says Marj. "If I remember correctly at that time I was attending a dance at the Orchard Inn at Ruislip. I had a late pass, ma'am."

In horns the W.O.1, vindictively. "Do you mind, ma'am, if I collect the pass book? We can soon check on that."

"By all means do so," says the O.C.

The late pass book being duly collected the figures showed that Corporal Marjorie Hayward had indeed checked in at 2359 hours. An hour and a half after the incident.

And the roster had been duly signed and attested by the corporal on duty watch for that particular evening.

There was nothing else to do but discontinue the investigation for want of any substantial evidence.

This is just one sideline story of gals at war . . . I wonder how many more the gals could talk about?

Cease Fire – 1918

I was in Mons on Armistice Day, 1944. Nowhere in the world does Armistice Day attain the full depth and meaning that it does in Mons — the ancient little Belgian city near the French border.

Almost everywhere else, November 11th is a bittersweet day, full of remembrance of valour and death; here in Mons, the day denotes the remembrance of valour and renewal of life.

Because all through the First World War Mons stood as a symbol of the great Allied retreat in 1914, and it was here, in the dark of early morning on November 11th, 1918, that the 3rd Canadian Division troops flung themselves upon the enemy for the last time in that war and regained, for the whole world to see, the starting point of the Kaiser's offensive.

Nor is the Mons celebration like that of any other city. The people do not stand silent for two minutes at 11 o'clock and then return to their everyday affairs. Here it is the biggest holiday of the year and one of the most solemn. Ordinarily life is at a standstill and the whole population parades to the cemetery to lay flowers on British, Canadian, French and Belgian graves.

At the cemetery at 11 o'clock I stood before the gravestones of the British and Canadian dead as the civic band played the Allied national anthems and the people heaped flowers so high that the gravestones were almost hidden from sight.

The Canadians who fell here just before the war ended are not forgotten. I walked by their graves and read their names: Private W. G. S. Bennett, 20th Battalion, 3rd Division; Corporal J. F. Farley, Lieut. R. L. Germain, Private F. G. Fisher — all of them died poignantly on November 10th or 11th.

They knew the effort must go on to the last minute, and as I examined the tragic date on their tombstones and contemplated that they might have lived if they had not realized the full extent of their duty, I knew that here was a lesson to all of us in this last stage of another war which was being fought for the same high purpose — freedom.

I came away from the cemetery with the Burgomaster of Mons, Victor Maistrau — a tall, military figure despite his 74 years — and I heard from his lips the brave, anguished story of Mons in the First World War. How the 4th Royal Irish Dragoon Guards met the first massed German attack near Mons on August 23rd, 1914, winning two V.C.'s but losing an uneven battle, and how the Germans held the people of Mons in a fist of iron through four endless years.

Then we came to the ancient city hall, the Burgomaster and I, and he walked quickly to the windows and flung them open. Here was the cobbled square, the Grand Place of Mons.

"Here was a scene I shall never forget to my dying day," he said. "It was 26 years ago but it is as vivid in my mind as though it were last night.

"I was only an alderman in 1918, but I sat in this office on the night of November 10th - 11th because the Burgomaster, Jean Lescarts, was ill. Early that night the Germans retreated to the north end of the town and were shelling the advancing Canadians. The whole population was awake, as I was, and I stood at this very window peering through the darkness.

"At five in the morning of the 11th — it was very dark — I saw the shadow of a man and the gleam of a bayonet advancing stealthily along that farther wall, near the Cafe des Princes. Then another shadow, and another. They crept across the square, keeping very low, and dashed north toward the German lines.

"At that moment I thanked God. I knew this was liberation. Then, above the roar of artillery, I heard music, beautiful music. It was as though the Angels of Mons were playing. And then I recognized the song and the musician. Our carilloneur was playing "O Canada" by candlelight.

"This was the signal. The whole population rushed into the square, singing and dancing, although the battle still sounded half a mile away.

"In the city hall at six in the morning I first met some Canadians and we drank a bottle of champagne together. We did not know at the time that this was the end of the war.

"The dawn revealed a strange sight in the square. The Canadian troops, exhausted from their long offensive, lay sleeping on the cobblestones of the square while all Mons danced around them.

"At two o'clock in the afternoon it was officially announced that the war ended that morning at 11. Our joy will never be forgotten. Neither will we ever forget our valiant Canadian friends who died so heroically."

The aged burgomaster closed his window as though he was shutting out an era. The light of reminiscence fled from his eyes and he sank in his chair exhausted.

It was later in the day, when I was warmly mellow from the pleasant hospitality extended me, that the wonderful significance of November 11th came to me.

I don't know of any day in the year that is so poignant, so full of heartfelt meaning to a select group of people as November 11th.

The sorrows, the hardships, the toil, the weariness and the joys are all embedded in hallowed chambers of memory.

I thought of our remembrance symbol, the poppy, and its significance to war veterans . . . of the servicemen who for centuries before us had savoured the same warmth of comradely association.

One could hardly forget Lord Macauley's immortal words when he wrote of the French under Marshal Luxembourg defeating the Anglo-Dutch at Landen in 1693:

> "During many months the ground was strewn with skulls and bones of men and horses, with fragments of hats and shoes, saddles and holsters. The next summer the soil, fortified by twenty thousand corpses, broke forth into millions of poppies. The traveller who, on the road from Saint Tron to Tirlement, saw that vast sheet of scarlet spreading from Landen to Nierwinden, could hardly help fancying that the figurative prediction of the Hebrew prophet was literally accomplished, and that the earth was disclosing her blood and refusing to cover her slain."

And then I switched to Colonel John McCrae's imperishable words as expressed in his poem "In Flanders Fields" which I will not repeat as all of you know it word for word. But there is another poem that also stirs me deeply. It is called "Red Poppies in the Corn" and the first two verses read like this:

I've seen them in the morning light
When white mists drifted by:
I've seen them in the dusk o'night
Glow 'gainst the starry sky;
The slender waving blossoms red
Mid yellow fields forlorn;
A glory on the scene they shed
Red Poppies in the Corn.

I've seen them, too, those blossoms red,
Show 'gainst the trench-lines screen,
A crimson stream that waved and spread
Thro' all the brown and green.
I've seen them dyed a deeper hue
Than ever nature gave,
Shell-torn from slopes on which they grew
To cover many a grave.

Holding a treasured spot in my Library of Memories is a despatch captioned "The Cease Fire" by Beach Thomas, the well-known war correspondent of his day. Beach Thomas describes a memorable scene on November 11th near Mons. He wrote:

"With an inspired sense of historic fitness the Canadians had sworn to be in Mons while the war lasted, even if it cost life. They owed its capture to the spirit of the Old Contemptibles. The 5th Royal Lancers shared the historic event with them and heard, twice repeated on a clarion, the three notes of the "Cease Fire" — repeated alongside the smouldering houses ruined by German howitzers.

"I saw some of the Canadians on the road to Mons at 11 o'clock this morning. While tired, starved refugees, who had hauled their burdens through two armies and some shelling all the way from Brussels, filed along the edge of the road westwards, two columns of guns, Red Cross lorries, cavalry, marching men and all sorts of transport, continued their steady, methodic progressions eastwards.

"The Canadians looked happy, but the steadfastness that has won the war was still the master attribute of these soldiers who, ready to meet any demands, went continuously forward in panoply — gas masks, tin hats, and the rest. 'It is too good to be true,' said a stalwart Canadian sergeant from Vancouver, and then with a 'Keep close to the right!' — an order that has won many battles — he sent the procession forward."

No Armistice Day would be complete without remembering the imaginative work of Padre David Railton who conceived the idea of the Unknown Warrior who rests in his tomb in Westminster Abbey. The remains of six unidentified bodies were taken from the plains of Flanders, the hills of Artois, from Picardy and the Aisne, which included areas fought over by the Royal Naval Division. While no official statement has ever been issued as to how the final selection of one warrior was made, it is popularly believed that an officer of high rank was first blind-folded and then led into the hut-chapel at St. Pol where rested the six unknowns.

With outstretched hand, the officer moved slowly about the hut until his fingers touched one of the coffins. The body thus selected became an immortal figure in British and Commonwealth history, and soon countries all over the world selected and paid homage to their Unknown Warriors.

In the midst of all this sorrow and poignancy we cannot forget that there were moments of exhilaration and joy. Nowhere is this more noticeable than in the spirit, the music and the lyrics of "Mademoiselle from Armentieres".

The rollicking music composed by British actor Edward Rolland and the captivating lyrics written by Lieutenant Gitz Rice of Montreal will live in Commonwealth circles as long as men don a uniform.

Who can fail to get a lift from:

"Mademoiselle from Armentieres, parlez-vous.
Mademoiselle from Armentieres, parlez-vous.
Mademoiselle from Armentieres,
She's never been kissed for fourteen years,
Inky, dinky, parlez-vous."

Gentlemen of this select group: I need not remind you of the years since that grey, drizzly morning when the bugles rang out their "Cease Fire" and a strange silence descended upon the long battlefields of France and Flanders.

No more fitting curtain could fall upon this humble effort to remember that far-off day than the message left us by the late beloved Canon Scott, senior chaplain of the 1st Canadian Division, C.E.F.:

"Ye who tread the borderlands of death,
Where courage high walks hand in hand with fear.
Shall ye not hearken what the spirits saith:
All ye were brothers there, be brothers here."

To which I add my most thankful *Amen.*

The Nursing Sisters: a fine Bunch

I was jockeying for position on the five o'clock bus when I saw a woman with two kids trying to edge her way down the crowded aisle. She didn't stand out in the mob. She was middle-aged and pleasantly plump in her flowered summer frock.

I stared again at this jolly-faced matron. Nobody else stared. She was just another housewife with two ordinary looking kids. I stared because I was trying to place her. You know how it is. You know a person, yet you don't. Finally a picture began to take shape before my eyes. I wasn't seeing a plump matron in a print dress but a smart-stepping nursing sister in khaki battle dress and beret.

It was Jonesy. She looked casually at me. She knew I was staring, the way you can be conscious that someone is looking at you. Not a flicker of recognition was in her eyes. I can understand why she didn't spot me. Somewhere along the line I brought back from the Strand a passion for that delectable filler — fish and chips. And you know what they say about fish and chips: Thirty seconds in your mouth, thirty minutes in your stomach, but thirty years on your hips. So Jonesy didn't twig the slim youth that used to be.

Nobody in the bus took a second look at Jonesy. Why should they? She was just another housewife hurrying home to get hubby's supper. But Jonesy had a record that no woman on that bus could ever hope to emulate. Jonesy was an alumnae of a Casualty Clearing Station "Somewhere in France".

There must be hundreds of Jonesies around Canada today, unknown but to their intimates. Now they are just another carriage pusher in a supermarket lineup. These Jonesies earned a spot in our hearts during the last war that time can never eradicate.

The C.C.S. that stands out most in my memory was among the first units to cross into Germany. It was part of a light field ambulance that was the first medical unit of its type to land in France. If I remember correctly, they landed at Courseulles in July, 1944. They opened shop at Sequeville-en-Bessen, which wasn't exactly noted for its tourist attractions. They were the first in Belgium and again led the way into Holland and Germany. I think the unit was mobilized in Winnipeg. Perhaps someone can put me straight on this.

The matron of this fine bunch of sisters was Captain Helen Sirrs of Toronto. Some of the girls with her were, I think, Mary MacIsaac of Halifax; Dorothy Knight of London; Helen Woodsworth of Edmonton and Eileen Corbett of Calgary. I have often wondered how they are faring in civvy street.

Women such as these deserve special citations. Thousands of wounded near Caen, Carpiquet, Livaret, Wally-Beauchamp, St. Nicholas, Capellen, Nijmegen and Walcheren passed through their hands. And, for good measure, 500 wounded Jerries taken from military and naval hospitals at Boulogne also owe them a debt of gratitude.

Anybody who has passed down the line after being hit will remember the sight of their strained white faces. Faces that hadn't closed an eyelid for days. Bodies that stood erect passing instruments to doctors in a tent as shells burst close by. Many a man broke under such conditions and was sent back, but very few of these girls were among the returnees.

I had, as you have had, many enjoyable experiences during the last show. But to me the most relieving and satisfying experience was to come out of the ether, bewildered and a little scared, only to be reassured by a cool hand on my forehead. The owner of this cool hand was a trim and businesslike nursing sister looking confident and capable. You leaned back in your bed because you knew then that you were in good hands. You weren't afraid anymore.

The girls of No. 14 Canadian General Hospital on their way to Italy had an unpleasant experience. Their ship was struck by a flying torpedo. They lost the ship. Worse still they lost all of their gear. It was told afterwards that twelve girls shared one lipstick. When that was gone they raised such a ruckus with their supply officer that he nearly had a nervous breakdown. They didn't object to their ship being sunk. They could tolerate shelling. But they were hanged if they were going to do without their lipstick!

I wish one of those nurses would write a book. She could probably tell more funny experiences than any author.

The bus jolted to a stop. The passengers made way for a plump little woman dragging two non-descript kids. A man grumbled as one of the kids trod on his toe. A few looked impatiently at Jonesy as if she was holding them from getting home. I thought . . . I thought it was a long way from Wally-Beauchamp. A long, long way.

The Tale of a Small Bird and a Great Man

RIGHT next door to us lives a man, a woman and a canary. Nice people they are and the canary warbles sweet and high. The odd Saturday night they invite us inside for pretzels and beer which we accept with pleasure, the Little Woman having a fondness for pretzels.

Me, I am fascinated by their canary. The little critter looks just like a bird I once knew. You fellas might like to know that a wee bird played a small part in keeping up the morale of a big man in the fairly recent not so little war.

Those of you who water-ratted your way up the Scheldt Estuary will remember that things slushed down for a bit. The terrain, the flooding and the rains meant advancing at snail's pace and morale slumped accordingly.

You blokes will recollect that our morale program was concentrated around our great leader, General Montgomery. As a morale-booster Monty did a superb job. His untiring jeep-rides from unit to unit reminding all that we were the best equipped and best trained army of our day, did a lot for our spirit.

We all thought we were pretty good, but here was the top-kick himself right on the job and saying so. And, I kid you not, but this general was batting a high average in victories starting from El Alamein onwards.

Now at this point the team wasn't exactly in a slump, but there weren't too many homers to yell about. The Jerry infield had tightened up considerably and his pitchers were pouring in some heavy stuff.

Part of the drill to maintain troop morale was to keep Monty in the public eye. Monty was seldom averse to assisting in this campaign, but he never would tolerate anything that wasn't strictly on the up and up. He looked upon such publicity as part of his job to provide leadership and to maintain his popularity with the troops.

Behind the scenes there was a group of Army public relations officers who now and then were expected to think up ideas to keep Monty in the public eye. I was drawn into this vortex and hereby hangs a tale of a small bird and a great man.

As I said before, things were dull all over. The photographers had shot Monty in his caravan studying his maps; Monty in his caravan relaxing with a book of good verse; Monty taking time out to feed his goldfish. There just wasn't anything new to shoot.

Came the day when I was summoned to the tent of my august colonel. "Smith," says he, "as a soldier you have many, many shortcomings. Sometimes I think it is a pity you aren't born a Schmidt and fighting for the other side. But I will say this much for you: I know of no one as capable as you when it comes to scrounging, stealing or liberating things without being caught."

I looked modestly at my feet and blushingly accepted this accolade.

"And so," the colonel continues, "I would like you to go to Brussels, see if you can rustle up a good singing canary . . . at little cost. I would like to present this bird to Monty. Do you think you could do so within 72 hours if I was to arrange transportation and a pass?"

The Old Man gives me the gimlet eye of appraisal. Meantime my corpuscles are racing madly helter-skelter. I am fighting hard to stop from jumping high and shouting, "Brussels, here I come! Vive la Bruxelles!! Garcon, make 'em doubles and an extra one for my dog, yipe!!!"

Well, sir, I reckoned I could handle the assignment so, with a straight face, I saluted, about-turned, and almost forgot to pick up a jeep for fear it would slow me down.

Need I bore you fellas with the sad details of my first 48 hours on the loose in Brussels? Sad, very sad indeed, gentlemen, I assure you. The only saving grace was my beloved colonel's astuteness. He sent a runner along on the third day to check up on my progress.

"On parade, Smith," says I, downing the last of La Reve d'Or's redeye. "From now on you are strictly for the birds."

There is one thing that most mortals have that old newspapermen haven't . . . that's money. But there is one thing that old newspapermen possess to a greater degree than their fellow-men . . . that's connections. Within the hour I had contacted an opposite number at the Belgium daily, *Le Soir,* that prints along la rue Royale. And within twenty minutes I was with him in a little bird shop near the Boulevard Adolph Max.

Did the proprietor have a smart canary that could sing right pretty?

"*Mais oui, m'sieur,* the very best, and cheap at only one tousan' francs," was the reply.

One thousand francs said the man! He might as well have said four million. After my forty-eight hours adrift I definitely had paid off the mortgages on such edifying establishments as *La Lapin Blanc, La Coquette, Le Diable Rouge* and similar educational institutions. But at the moment I couldn't raise a plugged guilder.

Now you fellas know that money was never a thing to faze a Canadian soldier. And so within twenty minutes I was in another small store a few blocks away just back of the Place de Brouckere.

"How much you give for this jeep coat," says I to the little man. "Sell it to ya for two thousand francs."

The Little Man looks out the window.

"Fifteen hundred francs?" says I.

He picks his fingernails as if I wasn't even alive.

"Twelve hundred?" says I.

He slowly turns. "I geef you one tousan' franc."

"Sold!" says I, peeling off my only warmth and comfort.

"And, a package of seegarettes," he adds.

"Take 'em," I snarl, and hustle off with the filthy lucre.

A day later I make the press camp and the Old Man pins me quick-like. "Where's the bird? Did you get a good one?"

"A good one, did you say, sir?" says I. "I'm telling you, sir, I got the very bestest from the Audubon Society itself . . . and he's the champeen of all Brussels," I blurt out as an aftermath.

"Good boy, good boy," breathes the Old Man. "I have an appointment with Monty tomorrow. See to it that the photographers are lined up. The papers'll love this."

Well, the show went off without a hitch. Monty appreciated the gift and the photographers had a field day. There was only one slight hitch. The Old Man got my "champeenship" qualifications a little mixed and told Monty the bird was the champion of all Belgium.

Several years flew by, the war was over and Monty came to Ottawa on a special visit. There was the usual show on Parliament Hill and afterwards a reception was held at the Chateau Laurier. Monty, of course, was surrounded by brass from near and far. Finally, after all the greats and near-greats had shaken hands with the great man, the ranks thinned out and a few ingrates like myself were allowed inside the hallowed circle.

"Sir," says I, "you may not remember me. But I was responsible for getting you that canary while you were in Holland."

"Did you really?" says Monty. "My word, that was a smashing bird! I called him Herbie after your funny cartoon in the *Maple Leaf*. Smashing singer he was, y'know. Champion of all Europe, I believe."

I gasped and passed down the line. Champion of all Europe . . . Zowie!

Forgive me, Colonel, I didn't mean it to go that far. Honestly I didn't.

A Revolutionary Proposal

JUST about now I feel like writing a letter to Mr. Diefenbaker. I think that he, as an old sweat, should evaluate the terrific news recently released by a Harley street specialist. Normally I shy away from doctors but this fellow on Harley street in London can be my head sawbones any day of the week.

This dedicated man by name of Dr. Charles Rob told the British Medical Association that the best relief for pain was *alcohol!* Speaking at a meeting at Newcastle-on-Tyne he said, "I don't mean anything pharmaceutical, I mean *whisky.*"

Thank heavens, at long last we have a man of great intellect. I clipped his hallowed words from the paper and pasted it right on our bedroom mirror. There, beyond doubt, is irrefutable evidence that a wee drap o'whiskie is good for what ails me. To which the Little Woman snorts, "Birds of a feather . . ."

Back to Mr. Diefenbaker. Now, sir, I think that you have an opportunity to make Canada's armed forces the greatest in the world. All this hullaballoo about joining the services hasn't worked out too well. Quit advertising, I say. If you follow up my outline, within six months you will be posting Military Police at the recruiting centres to keep them out.

The very first thing you have to do is to throw out the whole medical corps lock, stock and band-aids. With them their medieval collection of drugs such as dimethylamino-ethylbenzilate; chlorpramazine; iodipamidemethylgucamine and gantrimycin must go also. In their place, to protect our boys from undue pain, we must have medications approved by Doctor Rob.

I suggest that you start slowly and over the years build up your stock of pharmaceutical supplies. As a layman I would recommend large quantities of simple mixtures such as Scotch and Irish whisky. This will keep those of Imperial descent free from pain. A few thousand cases of rye. This will solve your prairie problem. Some gin and tonic for the CWAC's, WREN's, WAAF's etc. 100 cases of bourbon to encourage Americans to join up. And 99 hogsheads of rum for the Navy. But absolutely no vodka allowed on the shelves. We cannot permit fraternizing.

Now then, having dispensed with all of the doctors in the medical corps you will have the problem of replacements. Never mind a staff meeting, sir — just call on the Legion. All you need to do is to make all Legion canteen bartenders commissioned officers. They are veterans, they know what a serviceman requires for pain, and they are skilled in mixing their medications.

On reflection, though, it might be unwise to fire all of the doctors. Keep a few on hand for incidentals like brain surgery, tumours and internal haemorrhages.

The next move will be to get rid of the nursing sisters. At least those that won't conform. Off must come those archaic uniforms. In their place must come short, snappy skirts, tight sweaters with lots of rock and roll. Immediately patients' morale will soar.

First thing in the morning, instead of that horrible basin of water at 6 a.m. the hospital loudspeakers will go on. Down between the beds rock the new nurses singing in chorus, "Don't Be Cruel, dah, dah, de dah."

Each nurse as she rocks her way along the aisles carries a small tray bearing jiggers of gin, scotch and rye. Instead of the ribald, "Wakey, wakey, take your medicine," they would croon, "Love Me Tender, Love Me True" . . . followed by generous portions of "Oh Be Joyful".

Sick-parades would be joyous and happy occasions. M.O.'s would not look on good Canadian lads with suspicion. Stricken from the role would be words like "leadswinger", "goldbricker", "Monday Morning Virus", etc.

I can visualize a typical morning sick parade like this:

M.O.: "Well, well, well, and what can I do for you this morning?"

Private: "I have a pain in my stomach, sir. Can't keep my food down. Feel terrible."

M.O.: "Hmmm, ulcers, me boy, ulcers; that's what it is. Drat these Army cooks. Ruining my lads, they are."

Private (worriedly): "Can I be cured, sir?"

M.O. (heartily): "Cured? Well, I'd say that you can. But it means a liquid diet for you, my boy. Lots of rum, whisky and gin, washed down with Australian wine. Run along now to the dispensary."

Private (happily): "Yes, sir; yes, sir, indeed, indeedy-deed-deed. Feel better already, sir."

M.O.: "And stay clear of that ruddy water. Rusts your pipes out, it does."

Next case.

Private: "Good morning, sir. It's my bowels, sir. Not moving regularly. All tied up, I am."

M.O. (thoughtfully): "Hmmm, a clear case of constipation. Dyspragia no doubt."

Corporal, medic (eagerly): "How about a Number Nine, sir?"

M.O. (screaming): "My God, man, a Number Nine? You want to kill this patient?" Mutters to himself: "The help they give us these days. Heaven deliver me from those old relics of World War II."

Private: "I feel terrible, sir."

M.O.: "There, there, my boy. Nothing to worry about. Just take 12 bottles of good Irish stout. One bottle every hour, on the hour, and you will be O.K. in the morning."

Private (happily): "Yipee, this is my day!"

You don't have to take my word for all this, Mr. Diefenbaker. If you recollect, this was standard procedure at the Battle of Trafalgar. A bloke got wounded, the M.O. gave him a noggin of Nelson's Blood, and the guy murmured happily, "Hack it off, doc, I'm feeling no pain."

If you have the time, go and see one of those Hollywood movies. Whenever there is a big Indian fight going on, do they send the wounded hero to the hospital? Not on your tintype they don't. A guy pulls out a Bowie knife. The hero takes a slug of corn-likker. Ten minutes later he is prancing around minus one arm and the other wrapped around the waist of a happy lass.

Y'know sir, I think that we really got something big this time. In fact, quite revolutionary, eh wot? Out with the old, in with the new. Away with calcium glucoheptonales, riboflavins and navobiocins. Let us see our valiant men treated with blessed pain relievers such as calvados au Carpiquet; cognac de la Rouen; vino mia Rosa; whisky hoot Argyle; schnapps du lieber; essence ze biergarten.

In no time at all you will see Marshal Zhukov hot-footing it over here to see his opposite number, Lieutenant-General Clark. All the Ruskies will be wanting to join the Canadian Army.

But play it quiet, sir. I hear they are looking for a new pain-killer over there now. It seems that Molotov cocktails have gone off the market.

I hereby bequeath on behalf of myself and my heirs this proposal, and all of this valuable information to my country . . . free of charge.

Quartermaster-General's office please note: All medals, decorations, citations and awards forwarded to me must have sufficient postage . . . or they will be returned.

... They Only Fade Away

I had a letter recently from a buddy on the prairies who sent a newspaper clipping about the death of ex-sergeant Michael James Hogan. It was sad news, because I knew and respected the old soldier very much.

I first ran into him about this time of the year at a recruiting station in 1939. You blokes will remember the feverish excitement when the war was declared — how the recruiting stations barely had their doors open when a mob of youngsters rushed in eager to do business.

Disappointments there were by the hundreds. Some had flat feet or weak tickers others weren't able to tell an E from a Z on the eye-chart. Apple-cheeked youngsters of 16 swore up and down that they were 18. Elders wearing the Mons ribbon stoutly protested that they were as good as ever.

One of the biggest problems facing any recruiting officer was Michael James Hogan. Tall and erect, with the bearing of a professional soldier, "Pop" as we affectionately called him swore to high heaven that he was barely 40 years old. He protested so loud and so vehemently that the recruiting officer passed him in the hope of getting Pop out of his hair and on to someone else's back.

To everyone's surprise Pop breezed through his medical. In his case they must have looked into his eyes, lowered two fingers and said, "Cough, please." Pop coughed and he was in.

The advance guard arrived overseas on Christmas Day, 1939. Pop was with this group. He was an acting corporal, unpaid. One week later he was a private. The familiar haunts of London town had proved too much for him. He went on a toot — borrowed paymaster's jeep, left said vehicle outside of an "educational institution" in Soho and was located therein by two burly M.P.'s.

I suppose the average age of the young bucks in barracks at that time hovered around 22. Anyone over 30 was rated as an Oldtimer. But to categorize Pop was another matter. He might fool the officers with his claim to only 40 years. But Pop as witnessed by us at 6 a.m. suffering from a hangover was no 40. He looked more like his late fifties.

The biggest problem we had with Pop was fitting him in on dates. We were all self-conscious about his age. Come Saturday night in the local pub and the boys would pair off. But how to fit Pop in? You couldn't honestly blind-date the old boy. He was old enough to be any girl's father.

Then Pop, in his soldierly manner, filled his own niche. It never occurred to us young bloods that Momma could possibly be at the pub with her daughter in any other role than as chaperone. To us an "old woman" of 40 meant a polite doff of the hat. The idea that Momma, too, might enjoy a little fun and games was something too preposterous to contemplate.

But Pop saw Momma through different eyes. With his military bearing, waxed mustache and ramrod back he caught Momma's eyes many, many times. It was then that Pop's popularity soared. Fellas came begging to him: "Hey, Pop, I have a honey over here but I can't shake her mother. How's about making a double date — puhleeze, Pop. I'll buy the drinks." Pop would look over the situation with the eye of a connoisseur and decide whether the project was worthwhile or not.

There are those in civvy street who might call Pop an old rake. But wars are not won by angels alone. On parade, Pop was a perfect soldier. "On parade . . . on parade; off parade . . . off parade," was his slogan. He had a burning desire to get away from parade and come to grips with the Hun. Although he never talked about his military past you could see from the way he handled his weapons that he had smelled powder before.

Pop really tipped his mitt the day he was given charge of our platoon for a drill session. The corporal was on sick parade and asked Pop to take charge. On occasions such as this no old soldier can resist the urge to show his wares. Long years of intelligent discipline, experience in dealing with men, pride of uniform and the Service, a meagre rate of pay, yet an acceptance of other intangible rewards — all these qualities shine forth.

And the boys loved it. They loved it because marching in perfect order, in beautifully-spaced ranks, with the arms coming up together and all the boots coming down together they sensed that here was a leader giving commands. A man who knew his men. With their rifles smartly at the slope they marched with pride and precision, in perfect ranks, in perfect step.

"PLATOOOON" . . . (we knew we were being watched by hundreds from many huts) . . . "HALT!"

The platoon cracked to a halt and held it. Not a man wavered. With the same precision they turned to their front, picked up the dressing, ordered arms and stood at ease.

Pop stood there in the middle of the drill square beaming with pride. And that was the beginning of his downfall. A lone figure crossed over the cinder ground. A straight figure wearing the crown and one pip of a lieutenant-colonel. It was the Old Man.

"Hogan," says he, "it is very obvious to me that you have handled men before. How many years have you been in the Service?"

Pop stammered and went into a flap. He tried to act the amateur soldier without much experience. But it was too late. The Old Man had him spotted.

The mills of the Army grind slowly but eventually they catch up. A month later Pop was called on the carpet before the Old Man. The colonel, doing his darndest to appear grim and military, had Pop's file in front of him. Between Ottawa and the British War Office records Pop's military history had been put together.

"Hogan," says the colonel, "did you ever hear of a warrior named Osman Digna?"

Pop started and flushed red. Osman Digna was a wild-eyed character who had caused the British much trouble in Egypt long before Nasser was a boy.

"And," continued the colonel, "did you ever hear of the Matabele War in South Africa? Could it be that you have knowledge of the Chitral Campaign on the Northwest Frontier? What do you know about the Relief of Ladysmith? How did it feel to smell gas at Ypres?"

Poor Pop just stood there paralyzed as the colonel read out the damning evidence. According to the records, Pop had first accepted the Queen's Shilling around 1888. He could be no less than 70 years old!

Pop tried to excuse himself by muttering that he was never much good at figures. They shipped him back to Canada, still shaking his fist at the blankety-blank fuddy-duds in the War Office.

The newspaper said that ex-sergeant Michael James Hogan was 87 when he answered the Last Post.

The Immortal Capture of Aachen

I don't know how you blokes enjoyed New Year's Eve but mine was a regular nightmare. A bunch of the boys dropped in with their respective senoras and they were nice blokes . . . all, that is, except Mike.

Mike the family man, Mike the old buddy that you shared your Woodbines with, is a pretty fair type. But Mike at 1 a.m. with eight good slugs under his belt is a guy with a perverted sense of humour.

The party was going along fine with much merriment. We had now passed the stage where you passed the drinks around . . . the bottles were there, so help yourself but go easy on the coke; there isn't much left.

It was at this point that Mike went over his depth. Possessed as he was about a skeleton in my closet and beaming with good-fellowship he hicced, "Say, Smitty, tell the gang about the time you captured a German city single-handed."

I stopped dead in my tracks. The cups of Oh Be Joyful left me cold. Mike had gone too far. This story was all dead and forgotten. Or was it? Can anyone ever live down his military past?

"You blankety, blank, blank, blank," I said. "If you ever breathe a word about this I will break every bone in your nasty body."

Mike just burped happily and smirked, "Go ahead, Smitty. Tell them about the time you captured Aachen single-handed."

The look on my face left no doubt that I had something to hide. The mob smelt blood and they wanted my hide. They got it. And Mike, that refugee from a kitchen fatigue party, wallowed delightfully in my misery.

Like a condemned man knowing his crime has been revealed, I now unburden my shameful past for all to hear and gloat over.

During the Last Great Unpleasantness I was the sole master of a jeep. This, plus a wandering licence signed by no less than General Ike himself, gave me permission to roam at will, to see and to report.

I was jeeping slowly forward behind the rear of the rearguard of the forward troops approaching Aachen.

By the looks of things ahead the place was kaput and it should be safe for me to enter. The only thing in the way was a division of our tanks commandeering the highway. So, young, stupid and impetuous, I jeeped hardaport and skidaddled down a side-lane to a short-cut.

A few kilometres later I began to realize that all was not well. There were no troops around and everything was deathly still. Noise I can stand a lot of, but this dead, dead silence, with not even a bird twittering, and in enemy territory, that can really get you.

Driving at about 5 m.p.h. I traversed a bend. At 3 m.p.h. I ran smack into four regulars of the Horst Wessel Bock Brigade who were in no yodelling mood.

They stared at me. I stared at them. What else can you do when you are frozen stiff inside? What would *you* do in such a situation?

Sure, I know what Smokey Smith, V.C., would have done. Hands up, bang, bang, bang. Hah! none of that counter-account embalming party stuff for this kid.

The staring continued. Neither party spoke. The Jerries, too, seemed flabbergasted.

It was then that I coughed. Oh, bless that nervous little racking hack!

At the cough, up went four pairs of hands and up went my heartbeat. The swastika boys were surrendering! Well now, well now, that was a bock of a different brew.

Out came the old equalizer. That trusty pard who had fought many a battle with me in front of a mirror at Brighton. That careless-hanging six-shooter that graced dozens of pictures to the folks back home. A real fightin' tool for a real fightin' fool.

Jerking my head the way Humphrey Bogart used to do it, I leered and steered the four Huns back to the provost centre.

To this day I don't mind a chest cold in the least. What if one of the Jerries had coughed before I did? Gad, what a horrible thought.

Later, in the flush of victory, aided and fortified by the courage of several cognacs, I retold the story of my heroism to my buddies. But by this time the four P.O.W.'s had increased to 44. By the time the graveyard watch went on I had half of a Nazi regiment behind barbed wire.

I wish the story ended there. My troubles with the Uhlans were small compared to what happened to me later.

Believe it or not — a crumb, a dolt, a village idiot from my own home town actually believed me. He actually did. He wrote home a vivid description of my heroics to his folks. By the time they got the story from him I was indeed a real fightin' fool.

His father, bless his hide, was a reporter. Delighted with a good feature story, plus the chance to play up a local boy, he went to town and printed the ghastly yarn.

Before he was finished embellishing the facts, he had Smith storming into Aachen ahead of the recce squad with a mouthful of grenade pins and a blazing Sten clearing the path. Hundreds of Huns were falling and surrendering. By the time the rest of the army had caught up with Smith, Aachen was in ruins beneath my iron heel.

Everybody got excited. The mayor wired Ottawa to send me home for a Victory Bond parade. My mother sent me joyous letters. Congratulatory messages poured in from friends at home. Right then I could have married the mayor's daughter and been appointed lieutenant-governor.

Fear and trembling was my lot for many weeks after Mother had sent me the clippings. Suppose the gang should find out about this frightful splurge of undeserved publicity? Life wouldn't be worth living.

Like all things, the affair eventually died down and the war went relentlessly on. But one night I came back to our quarters to find a group convulsed with laughter.

At first I was puzzled. They would look at something tacked on the wall, stare at me and go into hysterics. It was then that the awful truth dawned on me. Pasted on a piece of cardboard was a blazing four-column headline, complete with my picture, telling the story of my Aachen conquest. Subheaded was, "Local boy captures German horde single-handed."

Across the news story some witless creature had scrawled in red ink, *"Daredevil Smith, the Frontline Charlie; How I took Aachen in ten easy lessons."*

Oi, oi, oi, oi, oi! There she was. The whole shameful story from my home town sheet. Gazooks, what miseries befall the inflated tongue!

For months afterwards whenever a newcomer arrived he was informed in hushed tones that we had a real live hero in our midst. Moreso, I was invited many times to "Go ahead, Smitty, tell the man how you captured Aachen single-handed."

Oddsblood! 'twas enough to drive a man to drink.

If you ever notice a morose creature in the corner of a Legion hall sulking, take no chances . . don't mention the word Aachen in his presence.

They tell me that the man is dangerous.

Spud Murphy's Ghost

MAY the good Lord deliver me from *some* old army buddies. The good old days were good, but the ghosts still linger on. Ghosts like Spud Murphy who turn up to haunt me at regular intervals.

Of all the nogoodniks in the Canadian Army, Spud Murphy was the most nogoodnik of them all. Of course, there are some who say that I pushed him a close second. But just because I buddied around with the bloke and shared in some of his high-jinks is no reason to brand a fella for the rest of his natural. And yet, whenever I run into old sweats, the first thing they roar out is, "Smitty, you old son of a gun, whatever became of that sidekick of yours, Spud Murphy?"

Now I'll have you know that Spud Murphy was no buddy of mine by choice. He just sort of seemed to like the same kind of living and we fell into step together.

You know the kind. So you are broke and he's got two quid, so he hands over half. You do the same next time around. Nobody thinks anything about it.

Nowadays if I ask the character at the desk next to me for the loan of a five-spot, he looks at me like he's got a pain in his face and I'm asking him to go hock one of his kids.

Anyhow, I first ran into Spud at Debert. You couldn't think of a bleaker place to mate up with a buddy. Debert, you blokes will remember was a thousand acres of mud floating a range of Nissen huts at half mast.

You'll recollect that this was the jumping-off spot for overseas. The place where the troop-trains disgorged all the fightin' fools — the fightin' fools who had been given one week's leave, were recalled in desperate haste and then stagnated at Debert for three weeks waiting for a troopship.

Nearby was the friendly little city of Truro. Friendly that is, up to the point of frustration, trying to live with thousands of young bloods, all hell-bent on having their last fling before leaving for the great unknown.

So with masterly decision the powers that be regularly placed Truro "out of bounds". And just as masterly did the good troops ignore the order which kept the Military Police veddy, veddy busy indeed.

And so it was that two smarties named Murphy and Smith broke camp and proceeded to Truro. There, purchasing a delightful concoction composed of one mickey of rum, mixed with one pint of Australian wine well shaken, and jostled on the dance floor by hectic variations of the jitterbug, they experienced a feeling of rare buoyancy and ecstacy — a feeling of warmth and joviality not shared by two stoney-faced M.P.'s who seemed unaffected by tales of misery about attending a grandmother's funeral, but who kindly provided transport back to Debert in the form of a celebrated vehicle called the Black Maria.

The return welcome by the sergeant-major could hardly be termed heartwarming.

Next morning a grim-jawed C.S.M. barks, "Form up! Form up! Single file. Orders, orders SHAH! By-der-front, QUIMARCH, eft-ite, eft-ite, eft-ite, eft-ite, eft. Mark time — Halt! Left turn. Pick up your dressing. Stand still. Orders present, sir!"

A not too unpleasant Old Sweat of a major from the First World War then took over and listened to the C.S.M. rhyming off the charges.

" . . . Charged, whilst on Active Service, at Truro on 10th December, 1940, at 2300 hours, with being intoxicated and incapable. Also, whilst on Active Service at Truro on 10th December, 1940, at 2300 hours, using abusive language to an N.C.O., namely 84825, Corporal Richards, G. W."

"It's a bloody lie," blurts out Spud.

"SHARRUP!" barks the C.S.M.

The major looks reprovingly at the abject celebrators.

"No previous entries?" he asks.

"No, sir," says the C.S.M.

"Are you willing to accept my award?" asks the major.

"Sir," says I.

"You realize the gravity of all this?" says the major, shifting in his chair and fixing me with a sudden glare. "The charge of being absent from camp without permission is unfortunately an oversight not included on your report. That by itself is a drastic offence. The whole thing is a bloody disgrace, but in view of you having a clean sheet so far, I shall keep it in the company and not remand you for the C.O."

"Sir," says I.

"Seven days C.B.," says the major.

"Cap on, s'lute!" growls the C.S.M. "Orders, RIGHT TAH! By-der-front, QUIMARCH! eft-ite, eft-ite, eft . . ."

To this day the mere idea of my wife asking me to wash a few dishes sends me shaking and trembling from the room. For one week, for seven whole days and nights, in company with friend Murphy and several other disregarders of King's Rules and Regulations, I washed dishes for 500 troops.

I don't know what the Ordnance Corps or the Army Service Corps or whoever it is orders groceries for the army does in their request for grub. But if you have ever tried to scrape the glutinous jam from five hundred plates every night, you would conclude they get their raw materials from the glue factory that had the contract for army horses after World War I.

The pattern of conduct with Spud ran close to the same pattern for the next four years.

When the troops aboard the troopship had their tongues hanging out — Spud had a case of whisky.

When you couldn't get cigarettes in England and you snipped the butt and put it behind your ear for later on, Spud had a carton.

In Normandy, just when you were certain that bully beef was the only kind of food left in the world, Spud came up with a dozen eggs.

In Holland, as we slushed ankle-deep across the polders, Spud rode by on a stolen Volkswagen.

Eventually we parted company. For me a big operation was swapping an army blanket for a bottle of cognac. Spud got in the big-time league. He branched out on a wholesale basis — till the army caught up with him.

Thus parted the amateur and the pro, but not without some nostalgia.

The years rolled by. Like a ghost out of the past Spud showed up at my home one day. He was his old, affable, joking, free-wheeling self.

The only trouble was he was broke and out of a job. So what do you do? You invite a buddy in for dinner.

How do you tell the Missus and the kids that Spud is a nogoodnik? Spud, your old army buddy. And how do you explain that at one time you were almost a nogoodnik yourself? Only in those days the troops laughed at your antics, called you a regular hell-raiser and slapped you on the back.

And so the Little Woman beams to see an old army buddy in the home, the kids settle down for more of Uncle Spud's fantastic war stories and he stays for more than dinner. Four days to be exact.

By the third day the kids are in Seventh Heaven. Uncle Spud has not only built them a swing, two stunt bars, a see-saw but a small playhouse as well.

Me, I'm flabbergasted. "Spud, you shouldn't have done it. All that lumber. Let me at least pay you for the materials."

"Shucks, Smitty, it's nothing," says Spud in his big-time manner. "Just a little something for old times' sake."

Comes the next day and a loud knock at the door. Standing there is a grim-faced joker together with an even grimmer-faced policeman.

It turns out that Spud has, as he put it, "scrounged the lumber army-style" from a construction job nearby.

"Just like old times, eh Smitty?" he beams, in complete disregard of the consequences. "Once it used to be me and you and the M.P.'s. Now it's the civvy cops. Don't worry, pal, I'll pay 'em just as soon as I get me a job."

"Yeah," I says, feebly, as the neighbours peek through their curtains at the cop car outside my door. "Just like old times," and sadly I make out a cheque to keep me and my family out of the hoosegow.

Bless you, Spud Murphy. Bless you, and . . . goodbye!

The Story of Lover Boy

SOMETIMES I wish that I could be a woman for a few hours. Then I would see for myself how women size up a man as against a man's view of what women see in men.

That the two viewpoints are different is beyond question. Most men, bless 'em, have a personal egotism that secretly harbours a desire to be thought "quite a ladies' man". Failing to reach that exalted status we slip little darts and barbs into guys who seem to catch the women's fancy.

To sum it up, as the Little Woman puts it, "Some guys have got it; others — well, they just missed the boat."

This brings us back to the point, How do you know who's got it — and who hasn't? Hence my curiosity to be a woman for a few scant hours.

Certainly I would never have chosen Lover Boy as the female's pulse-quickener. I first met Lover Boy aboard the Scottish train as we left the small stone houses and rolling hills of Greenock far behind.

Looking at him in the dim glow of the blacked-out train it was obvious that this almost pudgy and craggy-faced character was nothing to write home about. His friendly blue eyes were about the only redeeming features I could comment on favourably.

How wrong I was. How little did I know about women. Six months after we had left the grey, dull, prison-like barracks of Aldershot everyone was calling this craggy-faced character Lover Boy. There just wasn't any accounting for it. From the barmaid at the Queen's Hotel to the ticket-taker at the cinema the girls brightened up visibly when Lover Boy spoke to them in his warm and friendly voice. And yet, never on any occasion did I see him try to make the first move.

Months later Lover Boy was on leave in London and I tagged along to pick up his crumbs. This was a dirty night in March. The weather outside was foul but inside the Cafe de Paris the smokey air was fouler as couples shuffled rather than danced.

Overhead a Jerry bomber with his engine shut off had slipped past our defences. The "wheeeeee" of his falling bomb was lost as the orchestra blared and the couples jitterbugged to *"Three itty fishes and a momma fishy too."*

Within seconds the Cafe de Paris was a complete shambles. Those who were reasonably mobile formed rescue squads to pull others from the rubble. Outside on the pavement Lover Boy held in his arms a scantily clad chorus beauty bleeding from a gash on her head. Tenderly Lover Boy wrapped her bare shoulders in his tunic and stayed with her until the A.R.P. boys took control.

Only those who were badly hurt could rate ambulance room, the rest had to make it to the first aid posts on their own. Lover Boy took this gorgeous gal with him for first aid attention.

From then on Georgette, the French chorine, and Lover Boy, the craggy-faced one, saw each other often. Whether at the Savoy or the Horse and Hounds, Georgette ignored the Hollywood types and had eyes only for our boy.

As most buddies do in the services, we drifted apart — me to my square hole in the Army system and Lover Boy to his.

Several years later I was stomping it up at the Beaver House in Brussels which was located, if I remember correctly, on the Boulevard Bischoffsheim. Beaver House, along with the Canada Club, was a place which politely advertised in *The Maple Leaf* that "partners are provided". Therefore, as one can well imagine, it was popularly patronized by blokes out of the line for a rest. Some rest!

Fellas, you should have seen the cookie enfolded in Lover Boy's arms on that dance floor. As they used to say in the services and probably still do, she was built like a brick you-know-what. Not only that, she was a well known Belgian movie actress who most blokes would gladly sign over their pay checks to for an indefinite period, given the chance.

Lyta Delville that night had eyes only for Lover Boy. She not only had eyes, she had a real yen for that bloke. So much so that when Lover Boy's leave was up in Brussels, Lyta dressed in a private's uniform and, head covered with a Yankee parka hood, drove all the way back to Nijmegen with him.

This was late in January of '45. Lover Boy's unit was based southeast of the Nijmegen bridge. The Jerries were watching from the other side of the Maas.

For days on end Lover Boy kept up his soldierly duties, but whenever possible he crept back to the basement of the old farm house where he brought rations for Lyta and petrol for the camp cooker to provide a little warmth. Everyone in the unit except the Old Man and his top staff knew the story. And to a man they kept Lover Boy's secret.

Early February, however, General Crerar changed all this when he began his great offensive with eight divisions of the Second Army plus three Canadian divisions and the 2nd Armoured Brigade.

With large areas flooded, the weather rotten, the ground thawing, soggy and terrible for tanks, Lover Boy caught his packet in the form of flying shrapnel.

How that Belgian girl ever got back unaided to Brussels we will never know. But months later I saw her again dancing gaily away at the Canada Club as if she didn't have a care in the world.

Lover Boy after several months in the hospital was given a job with SHAEF in Paris.

As all you blokes did when you could, I took my leave in gay Paree. Where to go in Paris? There were a million places. But francs, boy, francs — how many you got to spend, that was the BIG question.

My paternal guide at the Canada Club, which was just across the river from les Jardins des Tuilleries, slipped me an invitation to attend a reception at the Scribe Hotel where the fabulous Gertrude Lawrence was to be guest of honour.

At the reception I was chatting with this gorgeous and witty woman. After two minutes I knew she was with me in person all right but not in mind. Her eyes kept roaming around the room, continuously searching for someone.

You guessed it, mates. In the doorway there appeared Lover Boy. With an ecstatic cry Miss Lawrence rushed forward and cried, "Lover Boy! You naughty man, you are late for my party. I shall not excuse you until you have poured me a drink."

S'truth, fellas, you could have floored me with a pen quill. There was the homely galoot and the glamorous Miss Lawrence spouting away like people who have secret thoughts for no one else to share.

That was sixteen years ago.

In all that time I lost track of Lover Boy until one night recently when myself and the Little Woman were attending a dance at a convention. As the music stopped, there, standing in front of us, was Lover Boy, resplendent with a curvaceous gal who looked eligible for the chorus line at Radio City.

Of course the reunion called for a "few short ones for ole times' sake." The beautiful creature was Lover Boy's wife, complete with a mixture of French, English and Canadian accents and a scar across her forehead. Yes, she was the scantily clad chorine he had pulled from the rubble of the stricken Cafe de Paris in London twenty years ago.

"So that," says the Little Woman to me later, "is the famous Lover Boy . . . Hmmmmmmm."

"Yeah," says I. "Now would you mind telling me one thing. Just what do the women see in that homely, craggy-looking mug of his?"

The Little Woman muses for a minute. "Lover Boy," she says, "Lover Boy has got that indefinable something. When he looks at you, he makes you feel every inch a woman. I can't describe it and I feel foolish trying to spell it out. But, brother, has he ever got it!"

Gadzooks, forsooth, 'tis enough to drive a man to drink. "Garcon! another bowl of meade."

Those Troop Trains were Dull, Uncomfortable . . . but Fun!

I don't think a man has *really* lived unless he has been in the services during the war. For the horrors of war I am, of course, truly sorry. But for the experiences, the broadening, the complete understanding of what makes my fellow man tick, I have to thank the war. I am positive that every veteran in civvy street today has a broader and more tolerant outlook on the foibles and weaknesses of mankind than a non-veteran could possibly possess.

I could draw upon hundreds of experiences that typify how men are bonded together through comradeship, whether it be in the navy, the army or the air force. The methods may differ but the pattern emerges the same.

It is difficult to cite one phase of service life that is common to all three branches. However, all of you who signed on the dotted line for the King's Shilling will remember the troop trains, be ye navy blue, air force blue or just plain khaki.

Troop trains were undoubtedly the most boring and uncomfortable form of travel available. Yet, bless 'em, when you look back they were a lot of fun. A heck of a lot more fun than you enjoy today trying to squeeze through traffic or board a crowded bus.

Nobody loved a serviceman aboard a troop train. The despatching officers shoved you aboard with a sigh of relief — glad to be rid of you. The porters tolerated you. The waiters gave you the bored treatment as you tendered your pasteboard meal ticket. A troop train to them was a tipless nuisance . . . and so were you.

But mingled in with that there was always an air of excitement. Especially on that final trip. The one to the East Coast. You had travelled plenty before, but this was the Big One. Somewhere along the end of the line there was a big ship waiting. And somewhere in the hold of that big ship there was a hammock just for you. And somewhere on that big broad ocean was a German U-boat waiting, so it seemed, just for you!

You weren't exactly scared. It was as yet too remote. And besides it always happened to the other fellow. Never to you. Yet the prospect gave you room for thought. But you didn't show it as you laughed, sang and kidded with the rest of that boisterous gang.

Somewhere along the line the train was always picking up old chums — guys who had been in training with you. I remember one trip East starting from Regina. We picked up a bunch at Winnipeg. Last leave stuff.

You kidded the pants off the fellows who were kissing their gals goodbye. Nothing or nobody was sacred. One chap in particular was moon-sick over the sweetie-pie he had just left behind. It was pure suicide to let the gang see you wearing your heart on your sleeve. Immediately the mob would break into melody, "I wonder who's kissing her now, I wonder who's teaching her how" — with the emphasis on the HOW. Whereupon the poor unfortunate would either blow his top or else become glummer still.

Then there was one Lothario whose chick bid him farewell on the platform in no uncertain fashion. Man, she was chesty! If my memory serves me correctly, that gal made Jane Russell look like two badly bent pin-pong balls. The boys just about went wild as she threw her final clinch. For the rest of the trip the refrain kept up, to the poor guy's torment, "For I'm dancing with . . . in my eyes". No conscience, no conscience at all in that bunch!

Usually after the first day the train was dry. Anything in liquid form that came aboard with you unfailingly died a quick death. Then there would be feverish councils of war. The planning and the strategies for the next stop on the time table!

Was there a liquor store there?

How far was it from the station?

How long would it take by taxi? If not possible, did the taxi driver know of a bootlegger? How much?

Then the hurried forking-up, "Here's my two bucks."

Or, "Lend me five 'til pay-day, willya? I'm broke."

Not that the trip was one mad, exciting event. It wasn't. You spent hours just staring out the window — hours listlessly reading a bunch of words in a magazine that had little meaning for you. Hours more of just plain dozing or staring straight into space.

Truth known, most of the guys' thoughts centred on home. You secretly wondered if you would ever see home again. You couldn't get out of your mind the strained look on your mother's face as she said goodbye.

You were grateful to the Old Man who hadn't said much but who had slipped a ten-spot in your hand with a mumbled apology, "I wish it could be more."

You didn't want to think it, but you couldn't help wondering about your girl. Will she wait for me? You had told her to go ahead and have other dates, but secretly you hoped that she wouldn't have them.

Photographs were produced by the score. A photograph seemed the only remaining link you had with your loved ones. You showed the gang pictures of your girl. They showed you theirs. Whether the lass was comely or homely, the polite thing to do was to give an appreciative whistle. You made some comment like, "You lucky dog, how come you rate such a luscious dish?" The guy then put the picture back in his wallet feeling mighty good. And so it went all around.

Somewhere along the aisle of the train would come the click, click, click of the rattling bones. With them were the famous quotes in tones of eternal optimism.

"Come on baby, natch."

"Eighter from Decatur."

"Shoot the works!"

"I'm bust, anyone want to buy a good wrist-watch?"

Welcome breaks were the leg-stretching periods at the stations. Mad dash for the lunch counter where you begged to be served scalding hot coffee dregs along with the privilege of paying two bits for a stale cheese sandwich dying of old age.

Above the magazine counter would be scads of flashy silk cushion covers, all bearing endearing captions, "To My Sweetheart" . . . "Dearest Mother Mine", and so on. These you could have for a mere four bucks, or nearly three days' pay.

Gad, what a racket! The slushier and more tear-jerking the verse, the greater the sales. They tell me that certain jokers in Montreal and Toronto retired after the war filthy rich.

I can well believe it. They got eight bucks belonging to me. I now have two moth-eaten cushion covers around the house that I'd love to trade back for half price. Only I haven't the nerve. The good woman would scalp me!

Most troop trains wound up either in Debert or near Halifax. There, after you were bedded down, you began to wonder.

You began to wonder what the blazes all the rush, hustle and bustle had been about getting you aboard that troop train.

At the time of departure from your military depot you were shoved aboard like mad fiends.

The Hun was astride the Channel!

England needed every man! *You* were the one who was needed — not tomorrow, but right now, right away!

Then you arrived at Debert and sat on your fanny for three or more weeks doing blister-all but stare at the gumbo mud.

Horrible, boring days, weren't they? I wouldn't particularly care to go through them again. But then again I wouldn't have missed them for anything. Would you?

How Smitty Nearly won the War

UP with the rations this *ack emma* comes a letter from an old blanco polisher who used to play cribbage with me for high stakes. The loser always had to blanco the winner's webbing for one week.

Jake the cribbage skunker writes: "Smitty, every time I read your column I think you are a bigger liar than ever. Why don't you go ahead and tell the boys about the time you could have won the war single-handed."

A real wisenheimer is Jake. Every few years or so we get together and have a few bashes of army surplus anti-freeze. It is then that Jake insists I tell the gang about the time I could have ended the war months ahead if it hadn't been for the slowpoke brass.

Y'know, fellas, it's true, really true. I did hold the destiny of the world in my hands, but jealousy, fear and bigotry blocked my efforts.

Around about towards the end of the War the Old Man and I were jeeping near the outskirts of Oldenburg. Stopping to light up a Woodbine, the Old Man says to me: "Smitty, wouldn't it be a wonderful thing if someone could kidnap Adolph Hitler? With their leader gone, the Nazi machine would collapse and we could all go home."

"Yeah," says I, reflecting-like, "that's a great idea you got there, sir. I'll see what I can do about it."

"Crazy, man, crazy," says the Old Man. "Let's get back to Amsterdam while cook still has the kippers hot."

Later that night I got to thinking, why not kidnap the bloke? If I did this, they would surely give me a V.C. and I would be a ruddy hero.

So just before dawn I jeeped up to Zutphen where the fighting was thickest. Slipping through the outposts of the North Novas and the Chaudieres, I plunged into the Ijssel River and swam to the other side.

"Kaput! Kamerad!" I cried as a Panzer Division surrounded me. "Take me to your leader," I demanded. "I represent the United Paperhangers of North America. I have an important message for Herr Schiklegruber."

Hurriedly the Nazi brass made up their mind. Excitedly they jabbered. Ja! Der Fuehrer was a paperhanger. Perhaps this crazy man did have a message of vital importance.

Away I drove in a Volkswagen to Berlin. The Chancellery was in ruins. But below this was the *Fuehrerbunker* — fifty feet below the ground and built in two stories covered with a massive canopy of reinforced concrete.

Within a few hours I was shown into Hitler's private quarters. Excusing herself as a demure German *frau* should, Eva Braun quietly left the room.

There we were, alone. Alone, that is, except for a picture of Frederick the Great and Blondi, his large Alsatian dog.

"Fuehrer," says I. "I represent the United Paperhangers of North America. They offer you a truce. If you will sneak away from this way of life, they guarantee you a twenty-year contract as Chief Paperhanger for the White House."

I'll say this much for Adolph: he was no fool. Little did I dream then what he was thinking. Later he revealed these thoughts:

"Himmel! This Schmidt, this fool, this *weinerschnitzel* may have something after all. Those *dumkoff* Yankees all believe in democracy. They will do anything the unions insist on. If I pretend to take this job maybe I can strangle their whole army.

"To fight a war they must have maps. To read the maps they must hang them on a wall. If I can organize it so that only a union paperhanger is allowed to hang a map, I'll have them right by their shortitudes and their longitudes. Then I will call out all the paperhangers on strike and picket the Pentagon. Quicker than you can say *Uebergabebefehle fuer Deutsche Befehlshaber* I will have this war won."

With that Der Fuehrer does a little jig, shouting, "*Sieg Heil!* This is madness. It out-hesses Hess. But who knows?"

Turning to me, he says, "Schmidt, we go! Nobody questions my movements. I will issue safe conduct passes immediately."

Well, fellas, a day later I give the Old Man a snappy salute and report, "Sir, like you ordered, I kidnapped this guy Hitler. Now what do I do with him?"

The Old Man glared. "You been at my cognac again! Who is that funny-looking character you got with you?"

With that Hitler springs to attention. "Heil Hitler! I come in peace direct from Berlin and Berchtesgaden. I, too, am an old soldier — 16th Bavarian Reserve Infantry Regiment."

The Old Man just stood there, flabbergasted. "Smitty," says he, "I don't know what you have done, but this is a job for Army to handle. This we got to take to General Crerar right away."

Hours later we stood in General Crerar's caravan near Apeldoorn. The General too was nonplussed. He fixes me with a glaring look. "You blithering, blathering idiot," says he. "What did you go and do this fool thing for? This wasn't in my plans at all. Don't you realize that you have completely loused up my Order of Battle?

"These peacetime soldiers!" the general moaned. "Never, never, never will they learn to do things by the book. If I told Ralston once I told him a thousand times. No more ribbon clerks, please, just permanent soldiers."

Laying down his glasses, General Crerar makes up his mind. "This thing," he says, "is too big for me. General Montgomery at H.Q. 21 Army Group should handle this."

A day later, and there is Monty, Adolph and myself all closeted in Monty's caravan.

Downright cold and suspicious is Monty. Fixing Hitler with his iciest Sandhurstian glare he says, "Frankly, I don't believe you are Herr Hitler. Answer me this question: Who are, and what do you know about, Clausewitz and Moltke?"

"Never heard of them," says Adolph glibly.

"Hmmm," says Monty, "that figures."

"But," continues Adolph, I know a lot about you."

"Yeah?" says Monty, sceptically. "Just what *do* you know?"

"I know all about the NAAFI deal," says Adolph.

With that Monty jumps like a batman caught nipping his officer's bottle.

"How much *do* you know?" he says quickly.

"I know," says Adolph, "that you got an agreement with NAAFI to water down their mild and bitters, two for one, with the profits going to a home for retired Field-Marshals."

Monty goes white as a gin-fizz. "Who told you this?" he gasps.

"Oh, I got it from Arnhem Mary," says Adolph with a jaunty air.

"That frustrated disc jockey!" hisses Monty. "I'll jam her ruddy frequency, I will."

Monty, quickly gathering his wits, turns to me. "Smith," says he, "as Corporal Hitler has a contract to paper the White House and not Buckingham Palace, I rightfully believe this is a case for General Eisenhower's jurisdiction. Dismissed!"

Well, fellas, a few days later myself and Adolph, having hitched a ride with a Red Ball transport, finally made it to SHAEF in Paris.

I will say this much for Ike, he started off being the perfect gentleman. "If you are really Adolph Hitler," says he, "please answer me a few questions. Who won the 100 metres at the last Olympic Games in Berlin?"

"Jesse Owens," says Adolph.

"Then," says Ike, "how come you never showed up to present him with his medal?"

"How come you ain't got no coloured boys on your staff?" retorts Adolph, quick-like.

"Hmmm," muses Ike. "A sharp boy, this. The Republicans could use him in the deep South."

"You got a union card?" he continues.

Quickly Adolph produces his card in the Bavarian Paperhangers and Biergarten Slingers Union, affiliated with the International Union.

It is then that Ike loses his aplomb and the schoolboyish grin disappears. Frantically he turns to me.

"Smith," he cries, "do you realize what this means to me? Do you think that I want to remain a cruddy parade-ground basher all my life? No siree! Someday I am going to be President of the United States. And," he continues desperately, "if it ever gets out that I turned down a union man, I'll be ruined with Labour. Oi, oi, oi, oi, oi!"

And so it developed that we buried Adolph deep in the echelons of Aldershot. As the Russkies were friendly with us at that time, we changed his name to Karl Marxburger.

Karl went on to be records chief of a repat depot. Within a few weeks he had everything so fouled up that nobody got home for months and months. However, the brigadier in charge of the area said he seemed to fit into the system perfectly.

Now that you know the true story, you can disbelieve those tales of Adolph Hitler burning in his bunker in Berlin. He is living near me today.

I can't tell you his new Canadian name for fear of reprisals from Ottawa. They have threatened to cut off my five percent pension. "I know it ain't democracy," writes Andy Anderson, the new pension chief, "but that's the way the pretzel crinkles."

And that is the truth, fellas, s'help me.

Speaking of Ghosts . . .

DO you fellows ever have ghosts creeping up out of your past? It seems to me that whenever I turn, a character like Hamlet's ghost keeps popping up, reminding me of past wrongs and never lets my tortured conscience rest in peace.

You blokes may remember where old buddy Blackie dropped in out of the blue and nearly broke up my home, reputation and peace of mind with his ho-ho's, he-he's and haw-haw's of yester-year's activities.

The household had just about settled down, still viewing Father with speculative eyes, when, so help me, up crops another ghost of circa 1944; original place of habitation: Bruxelles, Belgium.

Feeling pretty good inside, I was leaving the bowling alley (having racked up a high single of 365; I won't mention the other two frames) when who should I run into but Jake Hogarth.

Why is it, I wonder, that in your lifetime there are some people that you will meet and never see again? Then there are others who, by hook or by crook, you will see every five or six years. You meet, have a small beer, kibitz a little, then away you go for another decade or so.

I last ran into Hogie at a Press Club show in Toronto. That was eight years ago. Prior to that it was early 1945 when His Majesty's Forces Overseas decided they had had enough of Hogie's peculiar way of life and shipped him back to Canada.

Now there were some guys who got shipped back to Canada and never got over it. Then there are guys like Hogie that you can't insult. Hogie was not only shipped back and given another chance, but within six months he had been re-posted to the H.Q. of a Military District and promoted — something he hadn't been able to achieve in three years overseas.

Adding insult to injury, when we all came back for demobilization, there was Hogie at the depot, outranking us all. I think when Robert Service wrote the lines, "There are strange things done in the midnight sun . . . but the queerest they ever did see," etc., he must have had the Army in mind!

And so when last month I again met Hogie I naturally had to "step inside" and have a small beer with him. I don't know, perhaps I am a sucker, but whenever I run into an old buddy, good or bad, I just don't seem to have the heart to give him the brush-off.

Anyway, there we were, cogitating over old times again. "How you doing these days, Hogie?" says I.

"Oh, this'll kill you," says Hogie. "I'm on the road selling for this soap company and I run into the sweetest chick you ever saw in this hicktown. So instead of checking in, I get 'lost' for four days. Finally, the district supervisor gets me on the phone, raises pure, bloody murder and tells me when I get back he's gonna fire me."

"Gosh, that's tough, Hogie," says I, with just the right amount of sympathy in my tone.

"Tough, hell!" roars Hogie, the tears rolling out of his eyes with laughter. "Two days later the supervisor gets a heart attack, and head office tells me I'm in line for his job. Whaddya think of them potatoes?"

I just sat there, flabbergasted. Here, if ever, was a man over whom an evil genie hovered, protecting him wherever he went with a cloud of good fortune.

And then I got to thinking about Hogie when he was with our unit in Brussels. The Old Man had tried him at everything, right back from the beaches in Normandy, and he had botched each assignment gloriously. Yet, always it seemed he was such a jovial character you somehow felt like giving him another chance. And so Hogie was put in charge of messing for our unit. The ordering of rations, barrack cleanliness, etc., was not a tough job, but Hogie loused it up as usual — beautifully.

And herein lies the tale. All ranks had been alerted that no less a personage than Defence Minister Ralston himself was to visit our unit. Orders came down from Echelon that we were to spare no effort in making the Minister comfortable. With him would also be the publisher of a large Canadian daily newspaper and two senators.

I don't have to paint a picture for you blokes of how things hummed around our unit. Vehicles were washed until they almost shone, barracks were scrubbed, clothes were pressed, web belts were blancoed and the Old Man clipped his mustache.

"Now," says the Old Man at a preview parade, "while the Defence Minister is with us, if I ever see any of you unshaved, sloppily dressed, or in any way out of kilter, Heaven help you! That'll be all. Dismiss!"

We all knew what the Old Man meant. We also knew that the Old Man was gunning for promotion towards red tabs on his lapels. This visit might conceivably turn the trick.

"Hogarth," says the Old Man, "I want to have a few words with you. I want the best damned luncheon for the Minister and his party that you ever dreamed about. Never mind the regular rations, get out and scrounge me some chickens, fresh eggs, crisp salads and all the trimmings. You follow me, Hogarth?"

Hogie read the Old Man loud and clear. He knew exactly where to go and who to see. A man like Hogie never had to bother with mundane things like money. He also knew the standard barter prices, just like a stockbroker on the Bourse knows the daily fluctuations.

Straightways to *la rue Radish* went Hogie in his jeep. This was the famous street in Brussels where the Black Market flourished. It was an illegal set-up forbidden by Belgian law. To protect the spirit of the law two gendarmes were posted, one at each end of the street. Along the street were the hawkers, with everything from fresh meat to army greatcoats.

Every hour on the hour the gendarmes would make a right turn and solemnly walk down *la rue Radish.* And every hour on the hour all business would regularly cease. Flaps would be pulled down over the merchandise. The gendarmes, with their Nelson's blind eye having seen nothing illegal, would then resume their posts, the flaps were pulled up and business proceeded as usual.

It is a matter of record that I never saw a skinny or ill-fed looking gendarme at any time on *la rue Radish.*

Within a few hours Hogie had bartered off his tea, soap and cigarettes for everything he required, including the most delectable Belgian pastries. When you consider that at that time a pound of tea fetched a good 10 dollars, a five-cent cake of soap 50 cents and lowly Woodbines anywhere from 10 to 20 dollars a carton, Hogie had plenty of purchasing power.

Back to the unit headed Hogie pleased with a job done in a manner which he relished and in which he flourished expertly. Jeeping along the Adolph Max, Hogie spied an establishment where he was well known. *Le Lapin Blanc* to Hogie was a home away from home. The good lady in charge was the Belgian counterpart of the jolly wife of an English pub-owner. But whereas the English publican pumped out mild and bitters, the Belgian hostess ladled out mild and pleasures. Hogie was susceptible to both.

Received with great gusto by the proprietress, Hogie downed his favourite concoction — a cognac neat, washed down by strong Belgian beer. This beer is truly special. There is a certain brand the Belgians use with hard-boiled eggs to cure hangovers. Personally I can recommend it. Two pints, taken early in the morning, will cure any hangover. The only difference is that you no longer feel any pain whatsoever.

Hogie, with good intent, had a few cognacs, followed by strong beers. Then he decided to have one more for the road. Only trouble was that he seemed to know a lot of roads and kept having one for each of them!

Several hours later Hogie had passed the point of no return. So what does he do? He throws a party. Back into the kitchen he goes, together with madame and the usual collection of hangers-on. Into the oven goes the chickens and fresh meats, and onto the table go all the goodies that Hogie had purchased for Colonel Ralston's luncheon party.

As always, the next day came. It found Hogie still in the sack at *Le Lapin Blanc*, snoring merrily away. Meantime the Defence Minister and his party arrived, did their tour of inspection and repaired to the mess.

The Old Man, blissfully unaware that things were not on the beam, escorted The Brass towards their table. The orderlies brought in the food and the Old Man geared himself for some pleasant compliments. Then he took one look at the table, and the blood drained away from his face.

Instead of the anticipated roast chicken with all the trimmings, there on the plates lay the usual goulash of compo rations. I really thought the Old Man was going to have a stroke. He just couldn't believe his eyes. Those red tabs of his kept fading farther and farther away.

In the doorway there appeared a poor, bedraggled character named Hogie, red-eyed and chastened. He took one look at the compo rations, shuddered visibly — went to his room, lay down and faced the wall.

The Old Man ate in sullen fury, doing his damndest to put on a hospitable smile. We all felt sorry for Hogie.

Came the end of the meal and time for departure for the honoured guests.

The Hon. Mr. Ralston stood up. "Colonel," says he, "since I came to the Continent I have been wined and dined in many messes. I have eaten, till I've been blue in the face, chicken and things that I well know are not on army rations. I can't tell you what a pleasure it's been for me to sit down and eat an honest-to-goodness army meal. You are to be congratulated. I like your unit. You run a tight show."

The Old Man just gawked. He simply couldn't believe his ears and nearly tripped over his ankles showing them out the door.

Oh, Hogie got hell afterwards all right. But, of course, in the Army there are varying degrees of hell. And with the Old Man's red tabs once again looming brightly on the horizon, his wrath to Hogie was visibly dimmed.

So long, Hogie! I hope I see you again in ten years time . . . or longer!

A Night in the Clink

YOU fellas now cloaked in the respectability of civvie life (your crime sheets, MFM 6's, etc., being a thing of the past) should not get the jolt that I recently received.

Kids, bless 'em, come up with the darndest questions and at the most unexpected times. I was browsing through an old war book when Doug Jr. pops up, "You ever been in jail, daddy?"

Gadzooks, fellas, that one really shook me. Muttering a hasty, "No, no, no, of course not," I buried myself deeper into the book.

S'funny what a guilty conscience will do to a bloke. That innocent question kept recurring and, bless my unblancoed gaiters, I *had* done a brief stretch in the clink.

A right narsty piece of business it was too . . . subject to the prejudice and order of . . . conduct unbecoming, etc. — all under that ruddy Section 40 which covered everything from kicking the colonel's dog to parking your chewing gum under the mess table.

How was it that I, a young stalwart in King George's pay, should fall into the arms of the law? Simple, me lads; 'twas a weakness possessed by all of you buckos in them days — *cherchez la femme.*

In this case it was a fair damsel of Lincoln city. Gallantly offering to escort her home after a NAAFI dance, she demurred that she resided a scant thruppenny bus ride away. Now that didn't seem a fearful thing in itself and I, Big Time Charlie climbed to the top of the double-decker bus loudly singing, "Bless 'em all, bless 'em all, the long and the short and the tall."

What I had not reckoned on was the fantastic distance the British transport system would take you in wartime England for a mere thruppence. As the city faded away and gave place to winding country lanes I grew slightly worried. As I stepped off the bus, worry gave way to near panic when the conductor told me that this was the last bus for the night . . . and it was not returning to Lincoln.

Gone was the romance of the evening as I began my weary trek back. Not only was I miles from nowhere; I was hopelessly lost, footsore, hungry and sworn off wimmen for life. "Cuss 'em all, the long and the short and the tall."

Hours later I stumbled into Lincoln. Nary a soul was in sight on the blacked-out streets. Not a hotel but was full up. Not a desk clerk tendering more than the usual sympathy they reserved for pregnant skunks.

Finally in desperation I hailed a friendly bobby on night watch. Good bloke that he was, he directed me to a police station.

Standing before a night constable with my dust-laden clothes I related my tale of woe.

"Ho!" says he. "A Canydian! Well, well, well! Got a sister living in Toorontow, I have. Name of Truscott. Maybe you know her?"

Desperately I vowed I did know a family of Truscott. Could well be that it might be his sister.

"Well, well, well," says he, beaming all over. "My, 'tis a small world, now ain't it?"

Expanding with comradeship towards a Canydian who could know his sister from Toorontow, he continued, "Mind you now, 'tis against regulations to take you in, but," and he stopped short with a big broad wink, "there's a bloody war on, y'know. Got to make exceptions, else we shan't win the bloody show, will we?" I nodded eagerly. "And so," he continued, "cell number three should be vacant. Follow me, my lad."

Gratefully I heard the clank as his huge key opened Cell Number Three and I slumped gratefully on the hard boards and elevated headrest.

As with all nights, there came the dawn. In this case it was well after seven a.m. when I awoke.

Looking around the cell I could see that it had harboured other men of the services in the past. On one wall was scrawled, "The R.A.M.C. will see you through." In angry words beneath some other soul had scribbled, "Bloody Poultice Bashers."

Hailing a passing guard I asked to be freed from my overnight billets. Shaking his head he passed me by. In desperation I shouted, "Hoi, there, let me out, I haven't done anything." This brought action in the form of a ponderous, slow-witted constable whose face looked like an advertisement for the beefsteak of Olde England.

Solemnly he declared that the night constable had departed. True, there was no charge laid against me . . . but then again he had no authority to let me go until the sergeant's arrival. The sergeant, it appeared, was a bit late this morning; he had been up all night on A.R.P. duty.

Following hours of pleading and a breakfast of wartime sausages manufactured in a sawdust mill, I persuaded him to telephone my station. Being a goodly son of the law, he ignored my plea to phone the adjutant but contacted the service police. Eons later they arrived with their scarlet armbands, peak caps, blancoed webbing to take "the prisoner" home. No less than a paddy wagon was my vehicle of deliverance.

Unshaven, dirty, dusty, an object of suspicion, this poor creature spawned by the Gods of War was dumped unceremoniously into the guard room, there to lie and reflect upon my sinful life for the next 24 hours.

Gad, they don't stand on ceremony in those ruddy guardhouses. Bang! at daylight opens my door. "Ten minutes washed-shaved-dressed," barks a ramrod pinned to the floor with iron heels.

"What with?" says I.

"Stantoattenshun and answer 'Staff'," says the ramrod. "Draw your razor."

Prisoners' razors, lined up neatly on a shelf, were issued for a cold-water shave. The blade issued to me was first used by Genghis Khan, later captured in the Holy Wars, used as a harness scraper at Waterloo and taken from the British Museum for World War II.

Three layers of skin later the ramrod barks, "You! you're for Company orders at ten."

"Staff," says I woodenly.

Later, with the other criminals, I line up outside the Orderly Room door. The C.S.M., giving us icy stares, suddenly bites, "Orders, SHAH! Cused-nescort, bydefront, QUEE-MAR! Eft-ite-eft-ite-eft." Gad, if a fella wasn't guilty he sure as hell felt it now.

In staccato terms the C.S.M. read off my charges in that "that accused whilst on Active Service at Lincoln on April 12th, 1941, at 1100 hours was located in a public gaol . . . improperly dressed, cetera, cetera."

Solemnly the adjutant heard my plaintive tale of woe. An old sweat of Vimy vintage, he kept covering his mouth with his hand as my poor benighted self unfolded the miseries of the night before. The C.S.M. was not amused.

Finally, feeling that this could not go by unchecked, the adjutant let blast in the damdest chewing-out I ever got before or since, married or unmarried. Winding up he said, "No previous entries?"

"No, sir," says the C.S.M.

"Are you willing to accept my award?" says the adjutant.

"Sir," says I.

"You realize the gravity of all this," fixing me with his steely eyes. "You are over here to fight a bloody war, not to go tramping all over England after hours with pretty girls. You bloody well could have missed a draft, and, if your bloody draft had gone off by boat, you'd bloody well have to wait until the next boat . . . might even be posted as a bloody deserter . . . AND you know what bloody well happens to deserters in wartime, don't you?"

I gulped and swallowed. Gad, first I miss a ruddy thruppenny bus ride home and now I'm a deserter.

"This whole thing is a bloody disgrace," he says, "but in view of you having a clean sheet, I shall not remand you for the C.O."

"Sir," says I.

"Seven days C.B.," he growls.

"Cap on, s'lute!" barks the C.S.M. "Orders, RIGHT-TAH! . . . Bydefront QUEE-MAR! . . . eft-ite-eft-ite-eft . . ."

I am telling you fellas it was no fun being a criminal in His Majesty's Forces in nineteen hundred and forty one.

Missing, but not Forgotten

DEEP in attic trunks from St. John's to Port Alberni are many faded photos of you heroes of democracy in action. Me, I've got a phobia for sneaking away every once in a while to rummage through those precious snaps.

One picture in particular intrigues me. It is a faded photo of myself and Doug Johnson of River Hebert, N.S., taken in flying togs. In it I am shown dramatically pointing one finger to the skies with a look on my face that would do justice to a bald-headed eagle. Gad, what a ham!

Standing out among the group photos is the homely mug of Memphis. Brother, there was a character! Every unit in the early part of the war could boast of some volunteer from across the line. Memphis was our pride and joy. He hailed from Tennessee and had a drawl that lingered like a smoke ring. I don't ever remember his last name. Memphis he was from the beginning and Memphis he was to the end.

This group picture was taken in 1940 on the steps of No. 1 Wireless School on St. Mary's Road in Montreal. Originally it had been a school for the blind. According to our rasp-tongued instructors our entrance there hadn't changed things one bit.

Memphis, a happy-go-lucky character, had no use for discipline, rules or regulations. He wanted to go overseas and fight. Outside of that, this business of right-turn, left-turn and about-turn was just so much malarkey and wasted time.

A guy like that was an instructor's nightmare but a serviceman's delight. Popular as all get-out in the unit, he took a shine to me. I only figured it out later that it was a case of opposites attract. Memphis was a top-flight poker player and I was a sucker for drawing one card to try and fill a straight.

It was after he had completely taken my first two pay parades that Memphis called me to one side.

"Smitty," says he, "why don't you quit these pasteboards? Everytime you open your mouth to bet I feel weak inside. Honestly, buddy, you're strictly from hunger." Then, like a patient parent taking a backward child, he showed me a few facts of life.

"In the first place, when you are playing against me you just can't win. Here, let me show you." He then gave me a bewildering ten minutes of picking an ace from the bottom of the deck, then to "dealing seconds", which is dealing from underneath the top card.

It was the same when shooting craps. The only time I ever shot a seven was on the second or third rolls. Memphis then showed me how to pick up the bones and hold them in my hand three and four uppermost. Pretending to shake them, he threw them on the table with a twist so they spun around but didn't turn over. Seven every roll.

"You still want to throw away your do-ray-me, buddy?' he quizzed Feebly I thanked him and swore off.

I'll say this much for Memphis: once he got to know his own gang he always played on the up and up. However, after Saturday night sessions in a smoky hotel room on Peel Street, he often returned Monday morning rolling in dough.

Life went serenely on at the Wireless School with its daily routine of Morse Code, flags, Aldis Lamp, aircraft recognition, sentry duty, parade-ground bashing, air to ground messages, battery studies, wireless maintenance, physics, theory, etc., etc.

Then came the flap. A signal from R.C.A.F. Headquarters in the Jackson Building at Ottawa. A distinguished bishop would be visiting No. 1 Wireless School to see his son, and would the C.O. do all possible to make his stay a pleasant one?

You guessed it, mates. The V.I.P. son in our midst was no less than Memphis.

Feverishly the orders went out from the Orderly Room to find Memphis. They wanted to make certain that he would be pressed, shined and ready for the visit of his distinguished father.

There was only one hitch. Memphis was not with his company. Memphis was in the clink. It seems he had had a difference of opinion with a corporal-disciplinarian about lying on the cold, cold parade-ground at six *ack emma* for push-ups.

The discip said some harsh words and Memphis replied with even harsher ones, coupled with a roundhouse right that fortunately didn't do much damage.

The C.O., in a sweat with Ottawa, protocol and State Department all breathing down his neck, hastily tried to remedy the situation by parading poor Memphis before him. Military wise, the C.O. had little choice but to uphold his corporal's actions. On the other hand it turned out that the corporal had made some very nasty remarks about Memphis's U.S. ancestry.

With Canada eager for U.S. volunteers and the good bishop coming from across the border, it gave the Old Man an out. He upbraided Memphis, give him seven days' C.B. (postdated after his father's departure) and took away the acting corporal's unpaid stripes.

His Lordship the Bishop arrived in a gleaming black Cadillac with an even more gleaming black chauffeur behind the wheel.

I never saw Memphis look so clean and pressed in all my life. After a tour of the barracks, the bishop took Memphis out to dinner, then retired to the home of a clerical friend.

The good man made only one mistake. He loaned the Cadillac and chauffeur to his industrious son.

In the wee sma' hours of the following morning the Service Police reported a chauffeured carload of airmen rollicking riotiously from house to house on Ontario Street East. Any of you who know this area can vouch that the establishments there were educational if not cultural.

And so, once again the Old Man was roused to advise what should be done. To arrest the men in the sacred precincts of the Bishop's car was bound to leak into the newspapers. This would not look good in print. It would NOT at all look good in Ottawa.

The Old Man groaned. "Send them back under friendly escort. I'll attend to them later."

But the devil looks after his own. Two days later orders came through for our posting to gunnery school at Mossbank, Sask.

They say that Memphis's papers followed him. If so, they certainly never caught up. Six months later he was reported missing on Ops.

Memphis — missing, but not forgotten.

Scrounging . . . a devious Science

EVERY now and then someone pops up with the question, "I hear that you are in public relations. Just *what* is public relations?"

Well, fellas, I reckon I could give you a long-winded spiel but, s'truth, it's often I don't know myself what it's all about. However, whatever measure of success I may enjoy in the grey-flanneled field, I owe a certain tribute to the Old Man of my unit. They say that necessity is the mother of invention. Well, to put it mildly, my Old Man was one proper bawstard who made you invent and produce necessities.

A real big-shot was my Old Man. At least he played the part of the big-shot and it was surprising how many people fell for it. Well, let's say they fell for it hard enough to give him his red tabs, which ain't exactly peanuts in our khaki-covered league.

It was only after the war was over that I learned what the Old Man had done in civvy street before '39. It turned out that he had been a sales manager for crews of salesmen who peddled waterless cooking utensils from door to door. I can well imagine how this gave him the necessary brass and gall to handle men without too much compunction for their feelings.

Anyhow, as I said before, my Old Man was a proper bawstard. I think he must have written his own dictionary in which words like compassion, kindness and consideration were stricken out. On the other hand, like a real production man, he was strong on words like success, results, achievement, etcetera.

Fall down on one of his assignments, and you wrote your own ticket to a holding unit. Do a good job for him, and out of the blue would come a 72-hour pass with a travel warrant.

A queer cuss, who would just as soon put his own father on latrine duty if he didn't measure up to standard.

So it was around about this time of the year in '42 that I stood before him in his Nissen hut at Box Hill, a few miles this side of Dorking.

"Smith," says he, "I'll put it to you straight. Christmas is only a few days away. I have been invited to have dinner with Sir Thomas Hawkins and his charming daughter Barbara. They have been very kind to me. I would like to repay that kindness. I have prepared a Christmas shopping list that I would like you to fill. Here it is."

I pick up the list, read it and go pale. It says:

One bottle Scotch.

Three sirloin steaks, two inches thick.

One tin Turkish cigarettes.

One pair nylon stockings, size ten.

In wartime England you might as well have asked for the plans for D-Day.

Not giving me a chance to recover my breath, the Old Man cuts in, "Here's five quid; see the adjutant, get a 48-hour pass, some transport . . . and get cracking!"

Rallying a little, I stammer, "Bbbbbbut, sir, this is impossible."

The Old Man raises one eyebrow. "Impossible? ? ?" says he. "I understand you know a cute cookie who does a buck and wing at the Windmill Theatre. I also know that you have been soft-soaping her old lady with tea, sugar and eggs from our kitchen. Now get t'hell out of here before I throw a court martial at you for purloining army property!"

Now, you guys see what I mean by a proper bawstard? The bloke ran his unit like a door to door sales outfit. He knew everything and everybody. Probably would never qualify for the old school tie at Sandhurst . . . but then again he did get his red tabs.

By now a desperate strategy was beginning to shape in my mind. And here, my friends, was how you operated in wartime U.K. when you had to take emergency measures.

In my pocket was the colonel's five quid. But to buy such goods as he demanded, money wasn't worth its weight in feathers. So you developed the cunning, the avariciousness and the deviousness of an Arab trader.

In nearby Leatherhead lived Marj of Windmill Theatre fame and her mother Mrs. Parkinson.

"Marj," says I. "I gotta have a pair of nylon stockings, just for 48 hours. I'll pay them back, honest I will."

"You gone crackers, mate?" says she. "Really, Smithy, sometimes I think you have gone barmy, simply barmy. I'll give you anything we have, but not my precious nylons."

It was Mrs. Parkinson, bless her, who — after a pound of tea — saved the day and kicked through with a pair of nylons on a lease-lend basis.

Jeeping to London, I made straight for the Horse and Dolphin in Chelsea.

Two gin and tonics later I drew Joe, the pub-owner aside. "Joe," says I, "I need two bottles of Scotch; desperately I do."

Joe looks at me with closed eyes. "I daresay you do, mate, and so do thousands like you. Ever hear there's been a war on?"

He starts to walk away. This is no time for niceties. I saunter over to Mrs. Joe who is beaming at the cash till. Flipping open my tunic in my best black market manner, I reveal the pair of glorious nylons.

I won't bore you with the details. Three minutes later the brow-beaten and muttering Joe is handing me two bottles of Scotch in a paper bag at the going rate of twenty-seven shillings and six pence each.

Now then — move number two. Two mild and bitters later, with a friend from C.M.H.Q. I locate the nearest R.C.A.S.C. unit where the meat rations are handled.

It's a funny thing about rations for troops. Never in all of my five years in uniform did I ever see or hear of a sirloin steak appearing on any table — other ranks' or officers'. And yet a cow does have steaks. So who to see? The colonel? The adjutant? Don't be silly. The key-man in any such unit is the sergeant.

Now, to approach a sergeant and offer him filthy lucre for the purchase of a steak is crass madness. He would either call the Military Police and have you arrested for trying to bribe a servant of the King, or he would boot your posterior so far up your back you would look like the Hunchback of Notre Dame.

You do neither. I flip open my tunic and there, staring at the poor, thirsty, prohibition-confined man is a Heaven-sent bottle of Scotch.

Thirty minutes and six steaks later I am wending my way down past Lyons' Corner House in Leicester Square. Nearby is a tobacconist's shop.

"I'd like a tin of Turkish cigarettes," I say to the tobacconist. With a resigned stare he looks at me, pitying-like. Then he peers at my shoulder flashes. "Oi, a Canaidyun! Well, well now that accounts for it."

I haven't time to argue, so I flip behind the counter, whip open my haversack and flash him the sight of a juicy, two-inch steak. The poor bloke's jaw drops, he slavers at the lips, and shakily he reaches beneath the counter for a tin of Turkish cigarettes.

One more call to make. This time at the Red Cross centre for U.S. servicemen. The corporal at the door gives me the, "Beat it, buddy. No Canadians allowed."

"I don't want to come in," says I, "I only want to get two pairs of nylon stockings, size 10."

The corporal's jaws tighten on his well-chewed cigar. "You shacked up with some broad?"

"No," says I, "I want them for my Old Man."

"Oh," says he with a leer. "You two goin' steady?"

This, fellas, is where public relations begins. You don't sock the guy. You carry on in the noble tradition.

Again I flip open my haversack to reveal the juicy two-inch steaks.

The Yank goes limp. His eyes bug out. "Brrrother! You just sit right down here. Don't you go away. I'll be back in two minutes flat."

Minutes later he and another corporal return and between them they have two pairs of good U.S. nylon stockings.

And so a few days before Christmas Day, 1942, I return to Box Hill and to my Old Man . . . mission accomplished.

"Good boy!" says the Old Man. "Good boy. You may have Christmas Day off." And he chuckles with his own peculiar sense of humour.

I turn to leave and am passing through the door when a voice barks:

"Hey, you! How about it?"

"How about what, sir?" says I.

"My change," says he.

Bewildered, I fork over four shillings and thruppence — all that was left of the five quid.

As I said before, my Old Man was a proper bawstard . . . and that's how I broke into public relations.

Those Stout Navy Fellas

THERE was a brisk wind blowing and under me the boiling sea was surging wildly. The luminous green waters went turbulently by, mocking the green contours of my pallid jowls as I assumed my favourite position hanging over the starboard rail feeding the denizens of the deep.

Four times in the last war I crossed that monstrous body of water known as the Atlantic. And four times a cry went out among the fishes from Halifax North West Arm to Scapa Flow . . . "Ahoy there, mates! Smith's at sea again. Put on your feed bags tonight." Codfish slapped their tails with glee, porpoises frolicked on the surface and even the lowly green lobsters scuttled from beneath the rocks to get in on his feast of the year.

I was born on the sea. I have sailed abroad on the rolling waters more times than Christopher Columbus and I am sadly resigned to the fact that I will never be a sailor. Hence I dread the means of travel that so greatly disturbs me. Yet, secretly I harbour a great admiration for the men who master this treacherous beast and tame it to suit their needs.

And so it was in the last war. Whether it was aboard a converted Norwegian whaler or on the mighty "Lizzie", I watched these sure-footed men through bilious eyes. And yet I could never fathom it out. Here was I, a son of the sea, nervous and sweating as the ship rolled. And there were striplings from Prince Albert whose closest claim to the sea was a ride on a prairie schooner . . . clear-eyed and enjoying every rock and roll of the shuddering screws.

Even years later when I saw that wonderful movie *The Cruel Sea,* I gulped and closed my eyes as the corvette *Compass Rose* took a bad smash as she hit a "green one" in the North Sea. There was the ship, pounding her heart out in those crashing seas. Her whole hull quivered for seconds afterwards and I crouched lower into my seat and quivered with her.

I don't think that even the navy boys themselves fully appreciate what a terrific job they did in the last war. The men in the three services often displayed courage beyond the call of duty. But the overnight transition from civvy street into the role of seasoned sailors is one of the marvels of Canadian adaptability.

For years it had been an accepted understanding that before you could become even an A.B. you had to put in considerable time "before the mast". To get a ticket as an officer called for years of "coming up the hard way". Yet, within a few short years thousands of bank clerks, farmers, truck drivers, college boys and salesmen were confidently taking large ships across thousands of miles of waters they had never seen before.

I always attribute it to the persnicketiness of human nature that I should become so fascinated by these men. At every opportunity I watched them at work, secretly longing to be among them, yet fully knowing were I called I would shy away like a startled deer.

My greatest distinction came when I invaded the lower decks of a Canadian destroyer docked near Londonderry. A Leading Seaman and several "killocks" solemnly bestowed upon me the title of "Captain of the Heads". I was pleased as punch at the time and wrote home the goods news. It wasn't until years later that I learned the awful truth. Don't ask me to reveal my shame, fellas. Ask some Navy type. He will probably bust a gut explaining.

I don't think that in the last war the Canadian civvy population really appreciated the work performed by the Navy at sea. This could be partly attributed to the policy laid down at Ottawa of overplaying "The Silent Service" angle. Consequently the Canadian public did not, until later in the war, get an opportunity to evaluate the good job going on around them.

In Great Britain it was different. The round cap, blue serge jumper, white-striped blue jean collar and wide-cut trousers were familiar sights to most Britons. *Mare Nostrum* was very close to them and for centuries her sons had guarded her shores with "hearts of oak".

The navy life was different than that of the other services. Men at sea lived a life of constant strain and discomfort. This was especially so in the early part of the war when they sailed in small corvettes, minesweepers and ancient destroyers. So a sailor on leave grabbed what taste of shore life he could find . . . whereas the army and airforce blokes could take their time, knowing full well they would be around tomorrow. It was for this reason that the good mother hens locked up their little chicks when the navy hit town. It was unfair . . . but it was often so.

I don't think that it ever occurred to these good mommas that at least ninety per cent of those "terrible sailors with a girl in every port" wanted one thing only when their ships docked — a home where they could take a real bath, sleep between clean sheets and have a home-cooked meal. Undoubtedly they made eyes at the gals. Every red-blooded serviceman did. But our Canadian girls were so cloistered by their mommas that "over protectionism" set in.

Note the difference of the English home that were thrown wide open to the boys. Not much to offer in creature comforts. But they were ever ready to share their last bloater with you. That is why tens of thousands of young Canadians married English and Scotch girls and forsook so many potential Canadian brides.

Again I lay part of the blame on Canadians overplaying the "silent service" angle. Security was one factor, general information another. The Navy played up its victories when ready but failed to get across to the Canadian family the real picture of the Ordinary Seaman.

If I remember correctly the seamen always slept in the foc'sle, the least comfortable part of the ship. When a seaman entered a foc'sle he struck the word "private" out of his dictionary. There was NEVER any privacy. His home was a hammock attached to hooks screwed into the low-deckhead. When the Quartermaster called him at 6.30 each morning he got up then or else . . . or else if he didn't he later stepped out into someone's porridge on the mess table below him.

Then, the big problem might be not to just find clothes to put on . . . but any kind of clothes that might be reasonably dry. The powers on land had figured that a duffel coat plus an oilskin made up a combination guaranteed to keep out any wetness. Hah! They never figured on how cleverly that Atlantic water could find its way right down your neck until it worked its way around inside your clothes.

If war did nothing else it surely brought out the best in men. These same O.D.'s, coxswains, P.O.'s, cooks, shipwrights, gunners and engine room artificers are now again bank clerks, timekeepers, farmers, fishermen, lawyers and vice presidents. You look at them today aboard a bus and wonder how ever did they do it. The main point is . . . they did it.

When the sun climbs over the yardarm, to you stout fellas of the Navy I raise my glass and toast, "Long may your big jib draw."

Big Toes and Army Boots

YOU fellas realize, of course, it was twenty-two years since you shaved the fuzz off your face, deepened your voice and walked into a recruiting office headed for parts unknown.

I was ruminating on this blessed event when my ruminations were shattered by the Little Woman. "Sorry to interrupt," says she, "but could I have twenty-two dollars? The boys need new shoes for back to school."

"Twenty-two bucks!" I exploded. "How come, eleven bucks a pair? That's as much as I pay for my own shoes." Patiently she explained that growing boys' shoes cost that much nowadays if you want shoes fit to stand up to kicking tin cans, climbing trees, etc.

"By golly," I grumbled. "Can't see for the life of me why these kids can't wear good solid boots. The kind we used to wear in the army. Yes, sir, they might not be much to look at but they sure wore well."

"Well, well, well," says she. "Now that is a mighty change of pace. If I remember correctly, you swore up and down in 1946 that as long as you lived, never, never, never again would you ever wear another pair of army boots."

Gad, these confounded women with their elephantine memories! Ask them to do a simple thing like mowing the lawn, and one day later they will swear to all that's holy they haven't the faintest recollection of ever hearing you make such a request. But stored deep in their weird cranium-machinery are statements you uttered and had forgotten years ago, only to be resurrected whenever they want to switch the attack your way.

Minus twenty-two bucks I settled down to re-ruminate. Sure enough, I remembered that years ago I did swear that never again would I wear a pair of army boots.

Me and boots in the army never seemed to get along well together. Other chaps could gallivant about in the roughest hunks of cowhide. But each time I put my feet inside their casings, there lurked a rough edge protruding just enough to wear my skin raw, or a tight corner gleefully waiting to clamp a pincer movement on my big toe, and hold on.

But there is more to the story of army boots than mere slabs of cowhide and cobbler's nails. For the army regarded the boot as a sacred object to be protected by that zealous and jealous guardian of the public purse — the Quartermaster-Sergeant.

I must admit in all fairness that this august personage had due cause to be suspicious. The average Canadian soldier figured that army life was just one long battle. Him versus the authorities. And any time he could outwit said authorities, within the bounds of fair tactics, of course, it was his God-given right to do so.

In line with this was a parsimonious pay-scale that forever left him in a state of pecuniary destitution. It is beside the point that had he been paid one hundred and fifty bucks instead of one dollar fifty per diem, he would still be broke.

So, forever searching means of improving his financial status, he hopefully looked to his wardrobe. In that limited field there was little he could dispose of. Khaki tunics, webbing and gas masks had little value on the civilian market. But boots, now that was a cow of another colour. In clothing-coupon-conscious England army boots were very, very acceptable.

Now and then an officer could scrounge extra service equipment from the Q.M. stores. But let him mention the word "boots", and deep clouds of suspicion would gather on the sergeant's face. Even the mighty colonel did not possess a key to the regimental boot store. So the boots remained locked up and the taxpayers interests were protected.

Came the day when we took to the hills, dales and downs of England for route marches. It was our lot to have one of those ambitious blokes from a rifle regiment as the pace setter. Not content with the regulation 110 to the minute, he had to step it up to 120 or 130. By this time an evil, lurking piece of leather had my big toe at its mercy, and along I hobbled painfully and haltingly.

Now you blokes must remember that it isn't a simple thing to drop out of a route march. First you must seek out the nearest lance-corporal and explain your predicament. The lance-corporal in turn will relay the news to the platoon sergeant who then must inform the platoon commander. This august omnipotence may or may not decide to obtain the opinion of his company commander in the matter.

It matters not by this time whether there is any skin left on your big toe; you still hobble onwards . . . onward, ever onwards. Finally permission is given for you to drop out and return to camp. But hold on, you are not to be trusted to return alone. You might lose yourself or your boot, so a corporal is detailed to accompany you all the way.

Now, the next step is to report on sick parade. This I do with a wonderful feeling that the rest of the poor peasants are bashing it out on the parade square.

The Medical Officer, bless him, seems to be perpetually suspicious that the only reason a soldier comes to see him is to escape parades. This toe of mine, though, sports a blister as big as a shilling, so he gives it a cursory look.

"Mmmmm," he mumbles, "a riboflozin of the upper contusum."

"I thought it was a blister," says I.

He gives me the disdainful look all M.O.'s reserve for the vulgar ignoramuses who call a blister a blister.

Minutes later, sporting a dressing on my big toe and a recommendation that I get a new pair of boots, I make way for the Q.M. stores.

Working at the bins are two Q blokes and the Q.M.S. "I'd like another pair of boots," says I cheerfully.

There was a dead silence. Three pairs of eyes looked me up and down as if (a) questioning my sanity and (b) my integrity.

"What's the matter with the pair you've got?" says the Q.M.S.

"They hurt," says I.

"They all hurt," he snarled and consigned me to a destination where only boots with asbestos soles would be of any use.

Three days later I am still hobbling about. "How come you missed parade this morning?' barks my platoon sergeant.

"Oh," says I airily, "I got a riboflozin of the upper contusum."

"You gotta what?" he yells. "I'll tell you what you got, wise guy, you got yourself an invite to a defaulters' parade."

And so I try to explain to the captain that I got a blister on my toe on account of my boots don't fit. The captain who had just been chewed out by the Old Man over the number of malingerers to his unit, cuts me off quick.

"Extra fatigues for not reporting sick to the orderly sergeant," he barks.

The next three days finds me, the pride and joy of my mother and two maiden aunts, utilizing my valuable war effort ignominiously scrubbing floors and shovelling coal.

Still no new boots.

One route march later and this pitiful object again hobbles campwards accompanied by a grateful lance-corporal who smokes my Woodbines all the way.

This time the M.O., bless him, blows his top. Caustically he asks my captain if he has nothing better to do than louse up his sick bay with splay-footed soldiers. And why in blazes can't the soldier get a blankety-blank pair of boots.

Helplessly the captain shrugs his shoulders. Anything else he can get, but not new boots. There he has no power whatsoever.

The blokes who devised the rules of war first decide how difficult they can make it for a soldier to survive. Then when he seems about at the end of his rope, they get a group together called a Board.

Solemnly the Board heard the testimony of the lance-corporal who had accompanied me on my limping way. The M.O. gave his professional assurance that I was suffering from "a riboflоozin of the upper contusum". The platoon commander also gave his evidence.

After much deliberation and examination of the torturous boot, the Board gave as its finding that "Private Smith's boots should be condemned and a new pair of regulation boots issued to him."

Gratefully I saluted, about-turned on my blistered toe and hobbled triumphantly to the Q.M. stores gaily whistling, "My country, 'tis of thee".

There are Cops and Cops

THE office Christmas party being over, steadfastly I climbed behind the wheel and pointed the radiator towards home. The fact that I had a few under the belt never fazed me in the least. To a veteran with a background of ten mild and bitters, driving a blacked-out jeep through the winding suburbs of London, this civvy street driving was strictly a piece of cake.

Musing thusly I was blasted out of my complacent reverie by the spine-chilling sound of a police siren. Gad! the bloke was signalling me to pull over, and dutifully and righteously I did so.

Up strolls a bruiser of a cop who gives me a hard look, and then in his most restrained and trained approach says, "You in a hurry, mister?"

"Why no, officer," I says in my most friendly and unctious manner.

"Well, then," says he, "how come you just drove through a red light back there?"

So, back I come with the old bromide that cops hear every hour of the day, "The light wasn't red when I crossed first, officer; it was orange and I was already into the intersection."

He looks at me with a pained expression on his face, scans my driver's licence and calmly takes out his book to write a ticket. Then as an afterthought he leans forward and stares hard, "You been drinking, mister?"

"Oh, just a couple," says I, nonchalantly.

"Yeah?" says he, hot on the scent of a second charge. "Just exactly how many drinks did you have?"

Now this, my friends, is a time when you have to think and act fast. A ticket for going through a red light is one thing, but a charge for impaired driving, well, that's nothing to fool around with.

Stalling for time, in desperation, I spotted the war ribbons on his chest. There were five of them. "Weren't you in Normandy in 1944?" says I.

"I was there," says he non-committal like.

And then the luck of the gods took over and an elephantine memory of mine flashed that cop's face back to a scene in Normandy in 1944. Hitting out in the dark I jabbed, "Weren't you with the Provost Corps?"

"I was that," says he.

"And," I continued, "weren't you on point duty just near the Dives River near the road centre of Trun?"

His jaw dropped and his ticket book went limp, "Yeah, I was," says he. "How come you remember me?"

S'truth, fellas, one could never forget that red raw roast beef of Old England face of his.

Pressing my luck I continued, "You remember the time when I crossed over the road in my jeep and you bawled the hell out of me for crossing in front of a convoy?"

Slowly the scene came back to him. "Well I'll be damned. Now I remember — it was August and it was hot and dusty as hell. You're the guy who gave me a slug from his water bottle and it turned out to be apple cider."

"Yeah, yeah — that's me," I beamed happily.

"Hot damn," he says, "it sure is a small, small world." Then suddenly realizing that he was a cop on duty he straightened up. "Well I guess if you can think that sharp and that far back you can still drive a car O.K. On your way, and for Cripes sake, take it easy. Nice seeing you again," he concludes as he puts his blue ticket book away, unsullied by the written word.

Now this sounds like an everyday episode that might occur to any of us when driving. But later, on reflection, I felt it had a deeper meaning. I suddenly realized that although there are flaws in our judicial system and some cops can be mean and nasty, the average Canadian lawman is a pretty sound character when compared with some in certain other countries.

Let me take you back to Brussels, 1944, to cite an example of the difference.

Along about December of that year you could buy most anything you wanted in the Black Market at Brussels. They actually had a special street, la rue Radish, where the black market flourished.

It was one thing that eggs, butter, meat, soap, cigarettes and silk stockings were sold on the black market, but to find that our own army newspaper, *The Maple Leaf,* was being peddled for five francs a copy was a little hard to take.

In some ways it was flattering, but as we only had enough newsprint to give out one *Maple Leaf* to every five soldiers, we certainly couldn't afford any copies for black marketeers.

The problem was to find out how the jokers were getting the papers. I knew that our boys were exchanging a little petrol on the side — for bottles of cognac — but they swore up and down that they never sold one copy of the *Maple Leaf*. As they were a good, hard-cussin', hard-workin' and square-shootin' crew, I believed them. So, where did we go from there?

Finally we hit upon the leak. A few weeks before, we had agreed to give for free one hundred copies each day to a Belgian war veterans' hospital. Each morning around five a.m. they were thrown on the hospital doorstep. Some character had got hep to the delivery schedule, waited in the shadows and skipped off with the bundle!

Later I jeeped down to a newsstand near Place de Brouckere which is right where the Atlanta and the Metropole hotels are.

There, bold as brass, was this newsie with his other papers, *Le Soir, Le Drapeau Rouge, Le Soir Illustre* and others, peddling off our little *Maple Leaf* for five francs, worth about twelve cents in those days.

Standing not too far away was a Belgian gendarme. All slicked up, he was in his blues, reds and golds with a sweeping cape. I wasn't quite certain at first if he was a cop or a South American general.

"Pardon," says I, in my best *voolay-voo-mosoor* French. "That man over there has been stealing our newspapers and I want him arrested."

The gendarme raises one eyebrow and shrugs his shoulders. "I am sorree, m'sieur, but zat I cannot do."

"Can't do?" I bellowed. "Why! that lousy crook has been robbing papers not only from us but from your own wounded Belgian war veterans!"

A haughty look comes over his patrician face. "I repeat, m'sieur, zat I cannot arrest him. I 'ave my duty here, and here I mus' stay."

"Screaming mimies!" I yell. "You mean to stand there and tell me that this crook goes free and that he cannot be punished?"

At that a light dawned in the gendarme's operatic eyes. "Ah, m'sieur, you wish him to be punish? Why you not say so in zee firs' place?"

And slowly he turns, walks over to the newsie behind the counter, reaches in, lifts the poor tyke by his necktie and bashes him one smack on the kisser.

Grandly he turns to me. "Zere now, m'sieur, he is punish; it is satisfactory, no?"

"Yeah," says I dazedly, "he is punish," and I stumble away, for once completely at loss for words.

When Smitty Visited Paris

JUST about this time seventeen years ago I was huddled over a Number One camp cooker trying to cheer a little blood into my grimy hands. Don't let anybody kid you about the sunny climes of Europe. Northern Holland can out-damp, out-shiver any place I have ever been.

Perched as we were this side of the Nijmegen bridge and bivouacked outside the walls of an old monastery, I was cynically whistling Red Newman's famous hit, "Oh, it's a lovely war—Once a soldier was sent on leave and he simply refused to go."

Just imagine anyone refusing to go on leave, I cogitated, when Slim barged in with a, "Hey! Smitty. The Old Man wants to see you. On the double, mate!"

Stomping my boots hard to shake my trousers into line and straightening my gaiters, I give the Old Man a snappy one-two, followed by my Aldershot special salute.

"O.K., model soldier," says the Old Man wearily, "stand at ease and never mind the play-acting." Looking at me straight in the eye, he fires, "How would you like to go to Paris?"

A tingling sensation went right up and down my spine. It was like saying to a kid, "How would you like a trip to the North Pole to see Santa Claus?"

Steady boy, steady, I says to myself. Don't seem too eager. There must be a catch somewhere. So I replied, "Paris, sir? I've never been there, but if you wish me to go I'll do the best I can, sir."

"Yeah," says the Old Man. "And just what would you do in Paris if I were to send you there on a mission to SHAEF?"

"Oh, sir," says I, right businesslike, "if I had the spare time, I'd just love to see the Arc de Triomphe and the Tuileries and the Louvre."

The Old Man gives with a snort. "Smith," says he, "you not only are a liar but a blinking hypocrite as well. Tell me," he continues, "when you were in London for four years, were you ever inside Westminster Abbey? The Tower of London? Kensington Gardens?"

Blushing a little I stammered a feeble, "No sir."

"In Brussels," he says, "did you visit the Grand Place or Girault's Cinquantenaire?" Continuing relentlessly, "When we were in Antwerp, did you visit the Cathedral of Notre Dame? The Castle of the

Counts in Ghent or the Basilica of the Holy Blood in Bruges?"

Shifting uneasily, I muttered something about being busy at the time.

"Busy, hell!" the Old Man snorts. "You could write a history on every pub, dive, cafe, or bistro in Europe, so don't give me that malarkey about wanting to see the Arc of Triomphe. However I have to get these documents to SHAEF, and as you are the one who will be least missed around here I am sending you. You can take Giraud as a driver. He speaks French and he might save you from the Bastille."

Again I give him the old one-two and about-turned so eagerly I nearly fell on my face.

"Oh, before you go," says the Old Man nonchalantly, "while you are in Paris you might do a small chore for me. My wife has been hinting in her letters about some of this smaltzy perfume. Here's five hundred francs. Do the best you can, hey?"

I look at the Old Man. He looks at me. I get the message. The "do what you can" means only one thing: five hundred francs is all he is going to pay, so I am to see the Q.M.S., wangle a few cartons of fags for barter without the Old Man knowing it officially, and bring back a damn good bottle of perfume.

Within minutes I was packed—razor, toothbrush, clean pair of socks. Within the hour Jerry Giraud was jeeping me towards that wondrous city of beauty and sin, sin and beauty, sin, sin, sin . . .

"Oh, how are you gonna keep 'em down on the farm after they've seen Paree?"

You fellas every try to find your way around Paris? All streets are built on a curve or angle idea, with no such a thing as going straight. Giraud, it turns out, speaks French like a deaf mute and the only thing French about him is his name.

Stopping a Parisian with your old "see voo play, moosoor" routine ends you up exactly nowhere. The wonderful English used to take you to the middle of the street and direct you over fens and downs, but after the French are through with you—brother! you simply can't miss it.

Hours later, my packet delivered to SHAEF, I set out with honest intent to see the Tuileries, only first I had to sample a few of the French wares. By the time I had ranged from double Napoleon brandies to Chateau Neuf my cultural ambitions had waned considerably.

"Ah! zee Montmarte, you must see zee Montmarte, m'sieur," wheezes a portly goateed waiter. And so, Montmarte it was.

In a narrow alleyway close to Place Pigalle we stumbled upon a real Frenchy-looking cafe complete with Toulouse Lautrec girly-girly posters outside. "Arrrrruffff," barks Giraud, "and aaaway we go, go, go!"

"Pardon, m'sieur," says the doorman—a shifty looking character in a red jacket with gold epaulets. "You see zat man over dere?"

We looked across the street and there, true to life, leaning against a lamp post, was a real Hollywood version of a Parisian apache, complete with striped sweater, tight pants and cigarette dangling from his bloodless lips.

"Ah, m'sieur," says the doorman, "I must warn you. Zat fellow ees dangereux. He wait here for you to be zig-zag and zen he will strungle you."

"He will what?" we both echoed.

"Strungle you, m'sieur," and with that he puts his hands to his fat throat and rolls his eyes like he is being choked to death.

"But, m'sieur," he continues quickly, "eef you will geef to me tree 'undred francs, I will geef eet to heem and he will go away nevaire to bother you."

Brother! This was a shakedown racket for tourists if ever we heard one. But Giraud was really on the bit.

"Hmm," says he, "this should make a real good match."

"A match, m'sieur?" says the doorman.

"Yeah," says Giraud, "my friend here, he is the official hangman of the Canadian Army. Strangles deserters every week, he does."

"A hangman, m'sieur? How you say zat in French?"

"Oh," says Giraud, *"la meme chose, le executioneur."*

"Mon Dieu!" gasps the doorman. "Mon Dieu! Sacre bleu! ! !"

Hours later we groped our way through the darkened Place Pigalle, but nary an apache was there in sight to "strungle" us.

With weary eyes we headed the jeep back towards cold and cheerless Nijmegen, each engrossed with his own throbbin' noggin'.

Passing through Antwerp a cold shiver ran down my spine. The perfume! the Colonel's perfume! Not only had I completely forgotten about it, but all I had left to my name was thirty-five francs. What to do, what to do? The Old Man would chaw me into raw hamburger.

It was Giraud, bless him, who saved the day. Stopping at a leave centre, he obtained from one of the hostesses an empty bottle of *Soir de Paris*. With my thirty-five francs and his twenty francs we bought a bottle of cheap perfume and poured it into the *Soir de Paris* container.

"Aha!" beams the Old Man later. "*Soir de Paris*—the very best!

Bless you, Smith, you scrounger you. The Little Woman will love this, she will, she will indeed."

Gosh, I'm sorry, Colonel, honest I am. But guys get desperate in wartime, especially if they don't get to see the Tuileries.

Promotion Complex

I suppose there were guys in the Canadian Army who got promoted once and then never again. Me, I reckon I held down the one spot in the services so long I was often mistaken for a Chelsea pensioner.

At the outbreak of war when most blokes didn't know the difference between a tent pump and a left-handed housewife, I was among the brightest of the lot. This accident could be traced to my training as a youth with a renowned group called the Church Lads Brigade.

The fact that I knew how to shout out with some authority stentorian phrases such as: "Squad . . . wait for it . . . Squad — SHAH! Move to the right in threes, RIHOIT TAH — Byderlef' — Quickmarsh!" followed by my bestest parade ground shriek, "Chin up, chest out, look to yer own height there! . . . eft, ite, eft, . . . cover down front to rear. Dressing, dressing by the left . . . Heads up, watch them arms — up . . . back, up back. Change direction left . . . LEHEFT WEEUL, eft, ite, eft, . . . Squad . . . HALT!"

Beaming, the powers that be quickly promoted me out of the rank and file. And it was there that my army clock stood still. It seems that outside of a pre-war capacity to shout "eft, ite, eft" in a soldierly fashion I had little else to offer in return for the King's shilling.

And so it was this way a few years later when my Old Man called me to his quarters fronting the huge parade ground square at Aldershot.

"Smith," says he, "in two weeks' time we are to be honoured with an inspection by His Majesty the King. I don't have to tell you how important that is," he says, fixing me with his arctic-cod blue eyes.

"I am informed," he continues, "that C.M.H.Q. will be sending along a photographer. They want a man to assist him with his equipment and take down names of the men he photographs. I cannot afford any of my good men so — do you think you can do this job without getting yourself into too much trouble?"

Nice guy, is my Old Man. All heart and understanding — with the sympathy of a South American cobra.

Came the big day and our unit was something to be proud of. All ranks loved it, blancoing, cleaning boots and polishing brass and weapons with gusto. With their rifles smartly at the slope they marched on to the square with pride and precision, in perfect ranks, in perfect step, arms swinging waist-belt high like linked shafts in a single machine.

I have heard some guys scoff at royalty, but I have known few soldiers who did not tingle with pride as they stood to attention to be inspected by a man so revered as the late King George VI. You could hear a pin drop as he moved quietly up and down the ranks.

There was one fly in the ointment. A big, stuffy colonel from C.M.H.Q., acting as a sort of aide-de-camp. Everytime the King stopped to talk to a private and the photographer tried to take a picture, the colonel would poke his beaming muzzle right in front of the camera.

It was getting so our unit wasn't going to have any photo souvenirs at all except stuffy boy and his smirking Haymarket fizzogg. The photographer looks at me and I shrug at him. How do you handle a situation like this with a full colonel?

The final blow arrives when His Majesty stops to chat with a young, full-blooded Indian from Northern Ontario. This was a picture too good to miss. But—who again was blocking the view, practically hanging on the King's shoulder? The stuffy colonel, of course.

Signalling to Jake the photographer to line up the shot, I quickly step in, deliberately walk on the colonel's toe and say in my most righteous tone, "Sir, I think we are in the way, don't you?"

His Majesty, bless 'im, lowers the corners of his mouth in a quick offguard smile, the colonel mutters something like "sorry" and steps back a pace. Jake the photographer then gets the most wonderful shot of King George smiling at the Canadian Indian soldier.

Months later, everyone who has joined up with me is so far ahead that I begin to look an old boy from a retarded children's school. Even my mother, bless her, begins to query in her letters, nicely-like, when am I going to get promoted?

In desperation I get myself paraded before the Old Man. "Sir," says I, after giving him my special Church Lads Brigade salute, "sir, if it isn't too personal, I was wondering if there was ever any chance of me getting promoted?"

The Old Man for once almost looked human. "Smitty," says he, "by now you are to me what an old slipper was to my grandfather—I've got used to you. But as far as promotion is concerned there isn't a darn thing I can do about it."

He then went on to tell me the sad tale. The photogenic colonel had not forgotten my stepping on his toe. Straight back to C.M.H.Q. in Cockspur Street he had gone and filed the longest adverse report ever to be put on any record, with words reading like "insurbordinate, insolent, conduct unbecoming," etcetera, etcetera.

Wearily I trudged back to my barracks long condemned since the Crimean War, flopped on the creaking wooden bed and stared vacantly at "Hut Standing Orders" which read in part:

"Boots will not be cleaned on the table."

"Rifles will not be cleaned on the table."

"Cigarette ash and ink will not be spilt on the table."

"The table will not be damaged in any way."

Defiantly, and to be recorded for posterity, I took my pig-sticking bayonet and scratched on the side, "D.W.S. 1943." One week later I was orderly-roomed, confined to quarters and docked ten shillings for barrack room damage. The pride and joy of the Church Lads Brigade had sunk to an all-time low.

Meantime plans for the invasion of Europe went blithely along. Men with names like Eisenhower, Montgomery and Crerar seemed blissfully unaware of the dynamic and military potential of this young hopeful.

Time flew on, the impregnable Fortress Europa broke down, and my unit was munching sour apples in an orchard this side of Carpiquet.

"Smith," says my Old Man, "I've got a job for you to do. We have been saddled with a British war correspondent who wants to write nice things about the Canadians in action. Get yourself a Bren carrier, and for God's sake don't let anything happen to him."

Hours later, myself and Mr. Harkley Heathcote, of a London daily newspaper, were tooling down the road towards Benouville. I wasn't feeling too happy about the assignment as the Jerries were directing their shell-fire from the Colombelles chimney lookouts. Even the burlap and canvas screens placed along the south side of the road to block their vision didn't help my jangled nerves too much.

But not so Mr. Harkley Heathcote. Freshly arrived by air from London that morning he was full of mad-cap ambition. Gad, sir, his readers were going to taste the blood of battle right in his imperishable words.

Tugging at his walrus moustache he sniffed the air with the enthusiasm of a soldier let loose in a distillery.

"Take me to the sound of the guns," he says. I gaped at him. The man was mad. He had the light in his eyes of the early Christians going to the lions.

Somewhere near Benouville, after we crossed the first bridge, the

Canadians were in the woods along the banks of the Orne. However, to get to the woods we had to cross a small clearing, definitely marked with the ominous signs of *Minen*.

"Forward," says the British warco.

"Not for this baby, Mr. Harkley Heathcote," says I.

"Forward," says he again, pointing ahead with his swagger stick.

"No, siree," says I. "I don't know what your plans are for after this war, but me, I hope to be raising chickens, not daisies."

Well, fellas, with that he jumps into the Bren carrier and highballs it alone across the clearing.

Yes, it happened alright. He struck a mine. Minutes later I dragged his cut-up carcass back . . . minus a good Bren carrier. However, he lived and wrote again . . . much later.

Months afterwards I was wining and dining in the Metropole Hotel in Brussels. The Old Man was nearby, feeling no pain. This was my chance to get in the old needle about promotion.

"Sir," says I, "now that I've upheld the honour of the unit and shown the old *esprit de corps* and stuff, do you think, sir, there's any chance of me ever getting promoted before this bloody war is over?"

The Old Man sobers for a moment. "Smitty," says he, "my hands are tied. Your old pal Mr. Harkley Heathcote, when he got out of hospital wrote a blistering, stinking letter to 21 Army Group in which he cited you for "cowardice under fire, dereliction of duty, and God knows what else. I'm afraid that it's all on your file."

Well, fellas, that's the sad tale of my ignoble effort to assist my King and Country—the soldier longest on the payroll with the same rate of pay since Wellington kept his batman with him for life.

Nowadays I have the promotion complex. Every time someone nominates someone for secretary of the P.T.A. I raise my cherubic face in hopeful anticipation.

Some day I'm gonna make it.